HERE
LIES

A GUIDE TO IRISH GRAVES

Maeve Friel

POOLBEG

To Paul Kennedy
With love always

❧❧

Published 1997
by Poolbeg Press Ltd
123 Baldoyle Industrial Estate
Dublin 13, Ireland

© Maeve Friel 1997

The moral right of the authors has been asserted.

A catalogue record for this book is available from the British Library.

ISBN 1 85371 713 4

Cover photography by Brigid Tiernan
Cover design by Poolbeg Group Services Ltd
Set by Poolbeg Group Services Ltd in Times 11/13.5
Printed by The Guernsey Press Ltd,
Vale, Guernsey, Channel Islands.

ACKNOWLEDGMENTS

First and foremost I must thank my husband, Paul Kennedy, who accompanied me on many of my field trips and uncomplainingly gave up countless weekends to grubbing around in churchyards. I was fortunate to receive help and encouragement from a host of other people, in particular from many librarians and local historians, but also bishops, vicars, vicars' wives, priests, politicians, museum curators, landladies, publicans, teachers, gravediggers, sextons, keyholders and fortuitously met strangers who plied me with more suggestions for inclusion.

In particular I would like to acknowledge the useful advice and assistance I received from Mr Annesley Malley of Derry, Rory Murphy, Nicholas Furlong and Austin O'Sullivan, Wexford, Helen Lanigan-Wood of Fermanagh Museum, Enniskillen, Kevin McMahon and Michael McShane of the Creggan Historical Society, Armagh, Deirdre Armstrong of Ballynahinch Library, Tom Doyle of Dun Laoghaire Local History Society, Brian McCabe of Johnstown, Kildare, Margaret Comer of Swinford, Jack Stuart of Edgeworthstown, Brian Freeman of Drumcondra, Mary Guinan-Darmody of Thurles library, Ivor Hamrock of Castlebar Library, Michael Costello of Tralee library, Lynn Buick of the North-Eastern Education and Library Board, the staff of the library of the Society of Friends in Dublin and the late Jim Kemmy TD and Kevin Hannan of Limerick.

A NOTE ON THE AUTHOR

Maeve Friel studied sociology at University College Dublin. She is the author of four prize-winning novels for young adults, *The Deerstone, Charlie's Story, Distant Voices* and *The Lantern Moon* and has contributed to several anthologies. Her short stories have been broadcast on BBC Radio and published in *New Irish Writing*. She won the Hennessy Literary Award in 1990. She currently lives in Dublin.

INTRODUCTION

In May 1940, during the Second World War, the writer Frank O'Connor and his wife Evelyn set off on their bicycles to visit old churches and abbeys in Ireland, a journey he described in *Irish Miles*. Somewhere near Croom they turned off the road in search of a ruined Cistercian monastery. A car overtook them, forcing Frank off his bike. Evelyn noticed it was a Garda car. Soon afterwards it passed them again, more slowly this time, and the occupants had a good look at them. Later, walking about the abbey, they came face to face with the two gardaí and realised they were being followed. That night they learned that the moment they had left their lodgings, the gardaí had searched their room. The landlord told them there were rumours flying about that they were German spies: there was no other way of accounting for a man and woman looking at deserted ruins in bucketing rain unless they were involved in some sort of espionage.

When my husband and I set off on our odyssey around Ireland to visit the same old deserted ruins and graveyards, we met a measure of the same incredulity that anyone would choose such a strange occupation as grave-hunting. In fact, there could not have been a better re-introduction to Ireland after the best part of twenty years abroad than this project. It has taken me to every one of the thirty-two counties of Ireland and provided the opportunity to re-discover the country. A country's burial grounds are a rich and enduring historical and cultural heritage, offering us insights into our social history and allowing us to recall lost lives, some famous, some infamous, some tragic, some eccentric, some comic.

The most ancient burial places in Ireland are those built by neolithic farmers around 4,000 years ago; the finest of these are in the Boyne Valley at Newgrange, Dowth and Knowth but there are similar, if simpler, passage graves at Carrowmore and Carrowkeel and, of course, the one known as the grave of Queen Maeve on top of Knocknarea in County Sligo. The whole country, in fact, is dotted with megalithic tombs, often in such spectacular and prominent locations that it is not surprising that some far-fetched associations have grown up around them. Antrim and Limerick both claim strong links with the Fianna and each proudly boasts an Ossian's tomb. The Antrim one is spectacularly sited on top of a hill outside Cushendall, the Limerick one a cairn on the summit of Seefin mountain (Suí Finn means "Fionn's seat") overlooking Glenosheen, the valley of Oisin.

These enigmatic and striking early grave sites are also known as "giant's graves", "druid's altars" or "beds". There's a Dermot and Grania's bed at Loughmacrory, County Tyrone, a Diarmuid and Grainne's bed, a wedge-shaped megalithic tomb up a remote stony mountain face at Slievenaglasha in County Clare, and a Dermot and Grainne's bed, a dolmen on Inishmaan in County Galway. Of course, none of these could be the tomb of the doomed lovers since all these early burial places predate the Fianna by almost 2,000 years.

Then there are the early Christian graves, the graves of a motley contingent of saints and abbots of the early church, many of which were sites of pilgrimage from ancient times. The sixth century abbess Saint Gobnait, who used to drive away unwelcome intruders with her bees, is buried in Ballyvourney in County Cork where people still do stations around her grave and holy well. Saint Brendan the Navigator died at his sister's nunnery at Annaghdown but is buried at the entrance to Clonfert Cathedral under a slab which is dotted with what look like the paw-prints of a cat, the explanation for which is as fantastic as some of Brendan's accounts of his voyages. And there's the ascetic Saint Ailbhe, an Irish Romulus, suckled by a she-wolf who had found him abandoned under a rock. His name *ail beo* means "living rock". Ailbhe is buried at Emly in County Tipperary, the oldest see in Ireland. It will come as a surprise to most people that Saint Nicholas lies beneath a very spectacular stone near Jerpoint in Kilkenny.

Next come the graves of Gaelic chieftains and kings and Norman lords, and close on their heels, the dead of all the sieges, rebellions, uprisings and staged battles that have marked our history in the last thousand years. King Dermot MacMurrough, the man who changed the course of Irish history by seeking the Normans' help, is buried at Ferns in Wexford. Strongbow, the leader of the Normans, is buried in Christchurch Cathedral in Dublin. Wexford, the county which saw so much of the fighting during the United Irishmen's rebellion in 1798, is strewn with the graves of the insurgents, like Bagenal Harvey in the grounds of an old ruined church at Mayglass near Rosslare and Captain John Kelly, "the boy from Killann", in Killann. A pit in Arbour Hill cemetery in Dublin marks the spot where fourteen of the leaders of the 1916 Rising were placed in quicklime after their execution at Kilmainham Jail.

My quest for interesting graves uncovered several curiosities. The splendidly eccentric Adolphus Cooke lies in an extraordinary beehive-shaped mausoleum in Westmeath, described by Peter Somerville-Large in *Irish Eccentrics* as looking "as if a giant bird had laid an egg end up".

Others have starker monuments. There are famine graves from the Great Famine of the 1840s in Cork, Kilkenny, Clare, Mayo, all over the country, many of them mass pits where thousands of emaciated victims of hunger were dumped without ceremony, others like those on Achill Island marked by a simple forlorn lump of rock.

The graves of so many poets, playwrights, novelists and short story writers are evidence of Ireland's rich literary traditions. The grave of WB Yeats at Drumcliffe in Sligo is already well known but I tracked down and paid my homage at the graves of dozens of others including Maria Edgeworth, Elizabeth Bowen, Somerville and Ross and a number of colourful Gaelic bards such as the blind Raftery, the murdered Eoghan Ruadh Ó Súilleabháin and the hapless Sean Ó Tuama who drank himself out of his inn and ended up looking after a widow's chickens.

I have also visited the graves of all those political figures whose lives continue to forge and sometimes to haunt present-day Ireland, from the teeming Republican plot at Glasnevin to the solitary isolation of Sir Edward Carson in Belfast Cathedral. Wolfe Tone's grave at Bodenstown is a virtual shrine for many but the final resting-place of Robert Emmet is much more of an enigma. Though weight of tradition seems to indicate that he was buried after his execution in an unmarked grave at Bully's Acre in Kilmainham, there are at least another three claims, some more plausible than others. The claim by Blennerville in Kerry makes for interesting speculation.

"The Irish Inventor" are not words that trip lightly off the tongue yet we have our fair share, some in rather unexpected areas. The beneficiaries of the Reverend Dr Samuel Haughton's invention certainly had no opportunity to thank him but they would have if they could. Haughton was the man who invented "the long drop" system of hanging which replaced what was until then a slow and cruel death by strangulation. It was based on a precise mathematical formula which calculated the length of the drop needed in proportion to the weight of the person to be hanged. He is buried in County Carlow.

Given the Irish love of travel, I should not have been surprised to discover so many illustrious explorers of Irish birth, among them Captain Crozier who perished on the last voyage by Sir John Franklin to discover the North-West Passage, Francis Chesney "the father of the Suez canal" and

Thomas Heazle Park, the surgeon on Stanley's expedition up the Congo.

And so it was my net widened as local historians, librarians, friends and serendipitously met strangers plied me with information about interesting graves in their locality. There were many stories of shipwrecks: the *Lusitania* torpedoed by a German submarine in 1915 during the first world war; the *Wasp* sabotaged by the "cursing stones of Tory Island" and the *Moresby* wrecked off Dungarvan in treacherous weather on Christmas Eve 1895.

There are murderers and victims of murder such as Ellen Hanly whose death inspired a novel, a play and an opera, and the dashing "half-hanged MacNaghten", the feckless gambler and abductor. I also found the subjects of two great Irish love-poems, the eponymous Art O'Leary of *The Lament for Art O'Leary* – buried in the abandoned Kilcrea Abbey – and Elenor Booth Kavanagh, "Eileen Aroon", in an overgrown cemetery on the outskirts of Bunclody in Wexford.

It was inevitable that I should be distracted by the odd epitaphs and inscriptions I came across and also by some that I did not have the chance to see for myself such as the badly damaged one said to be in Kiltennell graveyard in Wexford:

> *Here lyeth the body of Jane*
> *Redmond who depd this life*
> *Ye 12th Feby 1787 Aged 27 years*
> *How lov'd, how valued once, avails thee not*
> *To whom related or by whom begot*
> *A heap of dust alone remains of thee*
> *Tis all thou art and all the Proud shall be*

Poor Jane to have had such friends or relatives! And yet the very callousness of the stone has given her a sort of immortality for it makes us stop and wonder who she was and how she died. In complete contrast is the brilliant affectionate epitaph put up to Tim Costello "who lived and died a right good fellow", which I quote in full in the entry for Kilfergus in County Limerick.

The apogee of the grave monument was the Victorian era. The Victorians almost made a cult of death and were prepared to spend vast sums of money on grandiose monuments and mausoleums redolent of the deceased's wealth and status. (Who says death is the great leveller?) There was no standardisation of design so the newly built private cemeteries of the time like Friar's Bush in Belfast and Mount Jerome in Dublin display an enormous variety of large memorials, winged angels, classical temples, obelisks, urns and plinths with bas-relief ornaments and medallions, many of them in very dubious taste. Often they carry lengthy tributes to the virtues, real or imagined, of the deceased. In James's Street in Dublin it takes one hundred and twenty-two closely packed words to make a "short and humble" tribute to a John Bergin of the Angel Hotel, clearly a paragon of every virtue known to man. It is hard not to be amused by such follies. In the Glasnevin Cemetery section of Joyce's *Ulysses*, the caretaker tells a good joke about two drunks traipsing around in the fog trying to find the grave of their friend "Mulcahy from the Coombe". Eventually they come across it, a huge sepulchre with a statue of Christ that the widow has had put up. Blinking up at the statue, one of the drunks eventually says "Not a bloody bit like the man, says he. That's not Mulcahy, says he, whoever done it."

All these epitaphs, brasses, monuments, effigies, mausoleums, sculptured tombs or the stark pathos of a lump of rock over a famine victim provide glimpses into the lives of our predecessors. The love and respect that they held for the dead are preserved long after the dead themselves have been forgotten. Nowadays when regulations and by-laws restrict the wording, the material to be used and the dimensions of headstones, it is the variety of styles in older graveyards that lend them their enchantment. The craft of the stonemason is evident in the monolithic Celtic crosses, the finely sculptured altar tombs like the one in Straide, County Mayo, with its cheerfully smiling bishops and saints, the table top slabs richly carved with spirals and Celtic motifs and in the typical eighteenth century upright stones with winged angels in relief that mark the burial places of vanished generations of weavers, carpenters, grocers, inn-keepers and the sad roll-calls of their unnamed children "who died young".

Sadly, property development and the inexorable demand for more and wider roads make it inevitable that graveyards are sacrificed. But sometimes the reverse happens. In October 1996, workmen excavating the foundations of a new shopping complex in Mullingar uncovered the skeletons of thirty-five friars. Some of them were wearing shells, suggesting they had made the pilgrimage to Santiago de Compostela in Galicia. One of the poor men, discovered in a crouched position, was probably buried alive. A few months later in May 1997, the extent of coastal erosion in the Dingle peninsula was dramatically brought to public attention when skeletons were exposed in the medieval cemetery of Teampall Bán.

One of the pleasures in writing this book was the serendipity of going to see the famous grave and finding something else as well, like the wonderful Romanesque west doors of Killeshin in County Carlow or Clonfert Cathedral, County Galway. The misericords of Limerick cathedral are unique in the country. Made of black oak about 500 years ago, they are the choir seats which when tipped up have a narrow ledge on the underside where the choir could rest their bottoms during lengthy services, giving the illusion they were still standing. They are magnificently carved with fabulous animals, unicorns, gryphons, angels and other creatures.

Then there were the ruins of the Benedictine Fore Abbey in County Westmeath with its Seven Wonders, among them a stream which runs uphill, an ancient tree studded with votive coins and a well possessing curative powers for sick children. Indeed, bubbling up all over the place, there are holy wells to cure every ailment from backache to warts. Clay taken from the grave of a Father McGauran in Creevelea Abbey in County Leitrim is supposed to be a panacea for pneumonia.

It was also a singular experience to have a Sunday morning drink in The Holy Ground, surely the only pub in Ireland situated *within* a graveyard in what was once the sexton's house. There is another pub, Kavanagh's, popularly known as "The Gravediggers" in Prospect Square beside Glasnevin cemetery in Dublin, which is not actually *in* the graveyard but beside the rear gate. It opened in 1833 when Glasnevin was first built and its interior, yellowed with the tobacco smoke of 170 years, looks as if it is unchanged since then. Gravedigging was of course thirsty work so it was the custom for the gravediggers to bang on the wall with their spades before their break so that the pints of stout could be drawn and ready for drinking when they came in.

The varying lengths of the biographies do not reflect the importance or my personal regard for the personality involved. I have taken for granted that some lives are so well known and so well documented that they merit only a brief thumb-nail sketch; others, less famous or forgotten, I felt deserved a longer entry.

Omissions are inevitable. As Frank O'Connor wrote, "It would take more than one lifetime to discover the reason for all the ruins in Ireland." Similarly, it would take more than my lifetime to survey all the interesting graves in the country. Some graves have eluded me, despite the most diligent searches. And of course many Irish people had, from my point of view, the bad grace to die or choose to be buried abroad. Sir John and Lady Hazel Lavery, Kate O'Brien, Michael Dwyer, Richard Brinsley Sheridian, Oliver Goldsmith, the Fenian John Boyle O'Reilly and a heavenly host of other famous Irishmen and women fell into this category. For these I cannot be held to account.

In any case, I hope that seeking out these graves, by the ocean, in ivy-covered abbeys, on the sides of mountains, in new and ancient cemeteries, in city cathedrals, in abandoned country churchyards and on off-shore islands will give you as much satisfaction as it gave me and that among these pages you will be pleased and touched by the stories of such a diverse collection of gifted and extraordinary Irishmen and women.

CONNACHT

GALWAY

BOHERMORE

Bohermore cemetery in Galway city is the burial-place of a number of famous and infamous Galwegians. Most infamous of them all was **William Joyce,** better known as **Lord Haw Haw** (1906–1946), the fascist who broadcast daily propaganda bulletins from Germany during the Second World War. (His grave is just behind the prominent plot of the victims of a Dutch aircrash over the Atlantic ocean in 1958.) Born in Brooklyn to an Irish father, Joyce had been brought back to live in Galway as a child. He joined Mosley's Union of Fascists about 1933, but when he was expelled from this, founded his own pro-Hitler British National Socialist Party and moved to Germany from where, in the bogus upper-class accent which gave him his moniker, he broadcast a barrage of German propaganda. Trying to escape after the Allied victory, his distinctive plummy accent betrayed him. He was captured by British officers and sent for trial as a traitor – strictly speaking, since he was American by birth, he should not have been charged with treason, but he also held a forged British passport and this was his undoing. He was the last person in Britain to be executed for high treason. His body was re-interred in Bohermore in 1976.

Lady Augusta Gregory (1852–1932), the playwright, is also buried here in Bohermore, to the left of the Church of Ireland church. At the age of twenty-seven she had married the sixty-three-year-old Sir William Gregory and became mistress of Coole Park. After her husband's death in 1892, Augusta grew more radical, unhappy with English apathy towards Irish political and social affairs. She became friendly with William Butler Yeats and invited him and others to spend the summers at Coole Park in a sort of "rural salon". She helped him revise his plays, researched volumes of Irish myths and legends, and collaborated with him and Synge in establishing the Irish Literary Theatre, the forerunner of the Abbey Theatre. She was co-director of the Abbey for many years and also wrote many successfully staged plays for the theatre. Her home at Coole Park was demolished in 1941.

The short story writer and essayist, **Padraig Ó Conaire** (1882–1928), was a diminutive man as shown by the statue of him in Eyre Square, the main square of Galway City. Although he published many books, including *M'Asal Beag Dubh,* a Gaelic *Travels with my Donkey,* he chose to leave his safe civil service job, and lived more or less hand to mouth for the remainder of his life. When he died in a Dublin hospital, he is said to have had no personal possessions other than his pipe and tobacco. Ó Conaire is buried on the right hand side of the main avenue, the words *Fíor-Gael agus sar-ughdar* – "a true Gael and an outstanding author" – inscribed beneath his name.

Walter Macken (1915–1967), the novelist, is another member of the literary circle here in Bohermore. His epitaph reads: "People are the cornerstones of the world". Macken had started out as an actor and stage manager with the Irish language theatre, An Taibhdhearc, and later joined the Abbey Theatre in Dublin. He wrote several acclaimed novels, including the popular *Rain on the Wind* (1950). His grave lies a short distance behind the large high cross commemorating Sebastian Nolan, a benefactor who left a substantial legacy to endow the Magdalen Society in Galway, the charity set up to rescue "fallen women".

RAHOON

> *Rain on Rahoon falls softly, softly falling,*
> *Where my dark lover lies.*
> *Sad is the voice that calls me, sadly calling,*
> *At grey moonrise.*
>
> (James Joyce)

Rahoon, the other Galway city cemetery on the outskirts of the city, has rather more poignant literary resonance than its location would suggest. In James Joyce's short story, *The Dead*, Gabriel's wife remembers her young lover, Michael Furey, who died as a result of standing in the rain one night hoping to speak to her before she left for Dublin. In real life, the prototype for Michael Furey was **Michael Bodkin,** a young man who had loved Nora Barnacle, Joyce's wife, and who had died of tuberculosis in 1900. He was buried in Rahoon cemetery by the wall to the left of the side entrance. Joyce's poem, quoted above, "She weeps over Rahoon", commemorates him.

The same graveyard is the final resting place for the distinguished actress, **Siobhan McKenna**, (d.1986). Her name, written in Irish, "Siobhan Nic Cionnait, Aisteoir", may be difficult to find as it is at the very base of a Celtic cross under the names of other McKennas.

CRAUGHWELL

There is not a school-child in Ireland who has not learned the poem, *Mise Raftaire, an file*. The author, **Antoine Raftery** (c.1784–1835), is buried at the gable end of the church in Killeenan near Craughwell in what is now known as Reilig na Bhfili ("The Poets' Graveyard"). He was one of the last poets of the oral tradition – both Douglas Hyde and Lady Gregory are responsible for collecting and writing down his poems – and it was Lady Gregory's idea to erect the tombstone over his grave. Douglas Hyde called him "the most remarkable man of whom I found traces in the West of Ireland." Remarkable he may have been but not necessarily charming, being considered bitter and greedy by many who knew him. Born near Kiltimagh in County Mayo, he was blinded by smallpox in infancy and spent most of his life on the road, visiting houses to recite poems and play the fiddle. He composed many poems on Irish history and contemporary events such as the election of Daniel O'Connell and the Lough Corrib drownings in September 1828. Two other contemporary poets of Raftery, the Callanan brothers, are also buried in this same small graveyard.

BALLYNAKILL

The writer and surgeon, **Oliver St John Gogarty** (1878–1957), is buried at Ballynakill, halfway between Moyard and Cleggan in Connemara. He was the prototype for "stately, plump Buck Mulligan", the tenant of the Martello tower in Sandycove in Dublin which figures in the opening episode of James Joyce's *Ulysses*. In this episode, Gogarty/Buck Mulligan has an argument with Joyce/Stephen when he shoots at the pans above Stephen's head – clearly an invitation to get out. This incident ended the friendship between Joyce and Gogarty with Joyce determining to leave Ireland immediately. He wrote to Nora Barnacle the following day to ask her to go abroad with him.

Gogarty was a larger than life character. It is said that when he was captured by Republicans during the Civil War, he escaped by swimming across the Liffey and later presented two swans to the city as a token of his gratitude. It was Gogarty who carried out the post-mortem examination on Michael Collins after he was killed. Gogarty's home, Renvyle House, in Connemara, was burnt down by the IRA, but he reopened it as a rather eccentric hotel. In the 1920s, he wrote a memoir *As I Was Going Down Sackville Street*. He became a senator in the Irish Free State but, increasingly dissatisfied with Irish life, he moved to New York where he died. In accordance with his wishes, he was buried in Ireland. The inscription on his headstone reads:

> *Our friends go with us as we go*
> *Down the long path where Beauty wends*
> *Where all we love foregathers, so*
> *Why should we fear to join our friends.*

CARRAROE

Muiris Ó Suilleabháin (1904–1950), a native of the Great Blasket Island off the coast of Kerry and author of *Fiche Blian ag Fás* is buried in the beautifully sited graveyard of Barr an Doire in Carraroe. Of the three writers from the Blaskets, Ó Suilleabháin paints by far the most idyllic picture of life on the remote off-shore island, probably because he was still a young man when he wrote *Twenty Years A-Growing* and had not suffered the grinding poverty that Peig Sayers and Tomás Ó Criomhthain had known. His lively stories describe hunting for puffins, listening to match-makers and drinking bouts. The book was so successful that he was able to give up his job as a civic guard in Dublin and settled in Inverin in Connemara. He was drowned in a bathing accident there on 25 June 1950. His headstone, a Celtic cross, has recently been re-incised.

CLONFERT

Saint Brendan (484–577), the mariner monk, who may or may not have sailed to America in a ship built of tanned ox-hides, is reputedly buried under a stone slab just outside the magnificent west door of Clonfert Cathedral. The stone is unmarked except for what appear to be the paw-prints of a cat. The story goes that a nun, fleeing in terror from attackers, leapt from an upper window but, before landing, turned into a cat and therefore landed on her feet on the grave-slab, leaving the prints of her paws. This is no more fantastic than Saint Brendan's own accounts of his sea journeys as recounted in the medieval manuscripts *Navigatio Sancti Brendani Abbatis* which relate how Brendan and a group of fellow monks made a remarkable journey to the Aran islands, on to the Islands of Sheep (the Faroes), to Iceland and Greenland and the coast of North America, surviving encounters with ice-bergs, talking birds and sea-monsters. In one episode they had beached their boat on an "island" and had lit a fire to prepare a meal when the "island" began to shake and move. The sailors fled to their boat while the island, presumably a whale, swam off with their fire still burning on its back. In fact, despite the allegorical and mystical flavour of the narrative, Brendan's journey also reveals great maritime, technical and navigational skills and it is interesting to conjecture, as Tim Severin did when he and his crew set out to repeat the journey in a replica craft, that Saint Brendan may indeed have travelled to North America almost a thousand years before Columbus.

While in Clonfert Cathedral, look for the many other ancient grave-slabs now erected on the interior walls and also for the pretty mermaid, the smiling angels and the dragon figures on the arch.

Another monk-explorer is thought to be buried in County Galway too. On a very small island, Inchaghoill, on Lough Corrib, near the ruins of a little Romanesque church, there is a very distinctive rudder-shaped stone, the Inchaghoill Pillar Stone. This allegedly marks the spot of the grave of **Lugna**, no less than a nephew of Saint Patrick, and a renowned navigator. The island of Inchagoill can be reached by boat from Cong.

On 12 July 1691, a year after the Battle of the Boyne, the last great pitched battle on Irish soil took place when the armies of King James II of England and William of Orange met at Aughrim, a battle that left more than 9,000 dead and decisively changed the balance of power in Europe. It finally secured the English throne for William and his wife Mary, James's Protestant daughter, and led to the so-called Flight of the Wild Geese: the emigration of many of the Irish soldiers and officers to fight for the armies of France and Spain.

Many of the Williamite dead were buried at Clontuskert Abbey, near Garbally on the road to Clonfert, though there is nothing to indicate this at the site. Clontuskert is one of Ireland's many ruined abbeys and priories that are forgotten, neglected and off the "tourist trail". It has a lovely west door with carvings of four saints and, as is typical of the style of Galway abbeys, a mermaid.

Most of the Jacobite dead were allegedly left to rot where they had fallen on the battlefields. Some of their remains were eventually interred at Kilconnell Franciscan Friary, about six kilometres outside Aughrim, whose friars were expelled around this time.

Look at the rear for the angry inscription on the Trimlestown tomb, the grave of **Mathyas Barnwall**, twelfth Lord Baron of Trimlestown "whoe being transplanted into Connacht with others by orders of the usurper Cromwell died 17th September 1667".

Charles Chalmont, Marquis de St Ruth (d.1691), who had arrived only months earlier to take command of the Jacobite army, was beheaded during the battle of Aughrim by an explosion of chain shot. He is buried under the old belfry tower of the Carmelite monastery at Loughrea. (An award-winning Interpretative Centre in the town of Aughrim explains the Battle of Aughrim and its aftermath.)

Although it has no known connections with burials, visitors to this area should make the detour to see the Cloch an Tuair Rua, "the stone of the red pasture", more commonly known as the **Turoe Stone**. Dating from the first century BC, it is an intricately carved stone associated with pagan ritual and cult practices in the pre-historic Iron Age. It stands in a field about half a mile from Bullaun, near Loughrea.

LEITRIM

The only tangible evidence for the existence of the King Dobharchu, Ireland's only lake monster, is the rather vulnerable crumbling Dobhar Chú tombstone in Conwell Graveyard, four miles south of Kinlough on the main road south from Bundoran to Manorhamilton. The tombstone has a relief carving of a strange animal with the body and legs of a dog, but the paws and head of an otter-like creature. A human hand is thrusting a knife or dagger into the beast's neck.

This strange stone commemorates **Grace Connolly**, wife of Terence McLoghlin, who died in September 1722, apparently killed by the Dobhar Chú which came out of Glanade Lake and savaged her as she was washing clothes at the waterside. Her body was found by her husband with the Dobhar Chú "in repose over her mangled breast". He stole back to the house for a dagger and slew the monster. Whatever about the truth of the story, the stone used and the style of raised lettering are similar to others of the same period so it was almost certainly made around the time of the woman's death. A similar gravestone was erected over the grave of Grace Connolly's husband and brother-in-law in Kilroosk – it was still in place in 1918, although recorded as badly damaged, but it has since disappeared.

KINLOUGH

Most tombstone inscriptions in Irish graveyards are in Latin or English, though of course several other languages make occasional appearances. In the graveyard of a ruined church in Kinlough, County Leitrim, a slate gravestone marks the burial place of two Welshmen, **Thomas Jones**, aged sixty-one, the captain of the schooner, the *Idwal of Bangor,* and his nephew, also Thomas Jones, of Tynrhos Farm, Parish of Llanwenllwyfo (Anglesey) who lost their lives at Red Brae on the night of January 25 1868, when gales swept over the British Isles and caused several shipwrecks. Their grave has a Welsh inscription from the gospel of Matthew: *"Am hyny byddwch chwithau barod: Ianys yn yr aur ni thybioch y daw mab y dyn"* – "Therefore be ye also ready, for at such an hour as ye think not, the Son of Man cometh." The Welsh emblem of the leek is carved on the headstone.

CREEVELEA ABBEY

A horizontal slab showing a mitre, crozier and missal in Creevelea Abbey marks the grave of a bishop who must surely be unique in Irish ecclesiastical history since he was consecrated in a prison cell. **Thady O'Rourke,** Bishop of Killala, died aged seventy-six in 1734 after a most eventful and stressful life. A nephew of Counsellor Terence MacDonagh, (see Ballindoon, Sligo), he was born in 1658, entered the Franciscan Order, and was sent to Vienna to the Imperial Court of Prince Eugene. This was during the time of the penal laws when priests were outlawed and Catholics forced to practise their religion in secret. O'Rourke was nominated as the new bishop of the Killala diocese and returned to Ireland to take up the position in 1707 with letters from Emperor Leopold to Queen Anne requesting that he be allowed safe conduct to Ireland. The difficulty was to find another bishop to consecrate him. At the time there were only two other bishops in Ireland, Archbishop Comerford of Cashel, who was a fugitive with a price on his head, and Bishop Donnelly of Dromore who was in Newgate Prison in Dublin. O'Rourke managed to visit Donnelly in prison and was there consecrated bishop. However, he spent most of the rest of his life on the run, living under an assumed name, and in the most dire poverty. Towards the end of his life he was living in a cabin near the ruins of the abbey where he is now buried. The Latin inscription on the tomb was recut and deepened in 1883 when the grave was restored.

KILMESSAN

Thomas Heazle Parke (1857–1893), explorer and surgeon, is buried in the family grave at Kilmessan, Drumsna, County Leitrim. After his medical training, Parke joined the British Army and was posted to Egypt where he volunteered to join the explorer Stanley on his expedition up the Congo to relieve the Emin Pasha in Sudan. (Emin Pasha was a German doctor and naturalist who had become a Muslim and had been appointed chief medical officer of the southern Sudan by General Gordon. After Gordon's murder, Stanley believed the Pasha to be in mortal danger and organised the hazardous expedition to "rescue" him. They travelled over 1,000 miles up the Congo river and then deep into the heart of the equatorial forest to fulfil their mission before returning to the east coast of Africa.)

Parke kept a diary of the journey during which he had to deal with a smallpox outbreak, virulent ulcers, arrow wounds, dysentery and a host of other problems, not least the Emin Pasha's head fracture when Pasha fell out a window during boisterous celebrations. Of the 800 men who had set out on the expedition, scarcely 100 survived. In 1890, Parke returned to England where he received many decorations but his health had been completely undermined by the rigours of the journey and he died soon afterwards. The graveyard at Drumsna, only seven by eighteen yards, is reputed to be the smallest graveyard in Ireland. There is a statue of Parke on the lawn outside the Natural History museum on Merrion Square, Dublin. It shows him, splendidly moustached, leaning on his gun, his water bottle slung at his hip and his sleeves rolled up ready for any emergency, the very epitome of Victorian man setting the world to rights.

CARRICK-ON-SHANNON

Not only does Leitrim lay claim to the smallest graveyard, it also boasts the smallest chapel in the world, the Costelloe chapel on the Main Street of Carrick-on-Shannon. It was built as a mausoleum in 1877 for **Edward Costelloe** and his wife: their coffins are sunk in the floor and are visible through a glass frame.

MAYO

There are two communal graves in Kildownet graveyard in Achill Island, both harrowing reminders of the harsh lives led by the islanders until very recently.

In June 1894, 400 migrant workers, or tattie hokers, assembled at the pier at Achill to travel by hooker to Westport where they were to board the ship for Glasgow. Many of them were in their teens and it was to be their first summer tattie hoking, that is, working on the potato harvest in Scotland to earn the money needed to pay the landlord's rent. 120 of them embarked on *The Victory,* the largest of the hookers. By any reckoning it was far too many. All was well until about half a mile from Westport when they caught sight of the steamer which was to take them to Glasgow. Everyone rushed to one side of the hooker for a better look. Within minutes the boat had capsized, throwing the passengers into the sea. Some would have been killed instantly, knocked unconscious by the mast. In all, thirty-two people were drowned, mostly young girls in their teens. The following day, the bodies were returned to Achill in the tragic inaugural journey of the train line to the island, a steam hearse moving slowly across the bog to Achill Sound. It is not difficult to imagine the grief of the islanders, a tightly knit community united by the loss of so many of their young people. By common consent, the bodies were buried together. The spot has since been enclosed within railings and a stone monument erected.

In another corner of the same graveyard, but on the opposite side of the road, are the graves of ten more young Achill youths, ten boys, the youngest only thirteen, who were killed in a fire in 1937. They too had gone to Scotland to work on the harvest. On the night of 16 September, a fire broke out in the "bothy" where they were sleeping on a farm in Kirkintilloch in Scotland. They had been locked in for the night and could not escape. The bodies were brought back to Dublin by steamer and, in an ironic echo of the journey home of the drowned victims, were taken back to Achill by train. At the time of the Clew Bay disaster, the islanders remembered a prophecy by a Mayoman, Brian Rua Ó Cearbhain, who had foretold 200 years earlier that "carriages on iron wheels, emitting smoke and fire" would carry coffins to Achill at the beginning and end of a new type of transport. This grim prophecy was fulfilled by the deaths of the boys in the Scottish fire for the railway line to Achill closed down two weeks later.

The Irish Times, reporting the second of the disasters, wrote "In that common grave, fourteen feet by twelve, these ten young islanders lie – the latest sacrifice which Achill and the men of the West have to make in their effort to win for their families and themselves on the harvest fields of Scotland and England that living which their own hard, barren, native soil denies them . . . sacrifices to a system which exacts a heavy toll on the manhood of the West."

Kildownet graveyard is also dotted with the small low rocks that mark the graves of those who died during the awful famine years of 1845–1851, the most poignant headstones to be seen anywhere in Ireland, set in place by destitute relatives over the graves of family members who had died of hunger.

DOOEGA

Before leaving Achill, as you drive along the magnificent Atlantic Drive and negotiate its corkscrew bends, look out for the memorial on the hill just outside Dooega to **Thomas Patten** (1910–1936), a member of one of the International Brigades who fought in the Spanish Civil War. Patten is thought to have been one of the first to die in the 1936 Defence of Madrid against Franco. The monument says – in three languages, Irish, English and Spanish – that he died for the Spanish Republic and all oppressed peoples.

BALLISHOOLE

As you come into the town of Newport, you see a striking mural of a priest being publicly hanged. This commemorates the execution for treason of **Father Manus Sweeney** (d.1798), a rebellious priest who had trained in the Irish College in Paris and later acted as interpreter to the French forces who landed at Killala in the ill-starred rebellion of 1798 and who had come to Newport after the so-called "races of Castlebar" when the British troops were routed. Father Sweeney was captured, then released on the representations of the Protestant minister, but was soon forced to go on the run when the French were finally defeated. He was recaptured when hiding in the roof-space of a house in Achill and taken to Newport to be hanged. He is buried inside a railed enclosure in the abbey in Burrishoole.

STRAIDE

His own experiences of social conditions in the West of Ireland and the constant fear of famine or eviction led **Michael Davitt** (1846–1906), perhaps Mayo's most famous son, to agitate for land reform. He had been only four years old when his family were evicted from the Knox estate at Straide and their house burnt to the ground. They spent some time in the workhouse before moving to Lancashire where Michael started work at the age of eight. When he was eleven he lost his right arm as a result of an accident in the local cotton mill.

Davitt was the founder of the National Land League, a successful mass movement of resistance against rent increases and summary eviction, one of whose effective weapons was a policy that gave a new word to the English language, coined by a visiting American reporter, James Redpath. Captain Boycott was the agent of the Lough Mask estate for Lord Erne, an absentee landlord who was insisting on raising the rents of families already facing bankruptcy as a result of poor harvests and falling prices. The Land League ostracised Boycott, refusing to have any dealings with him so that in the end he was forced to bring in a contingent of Orangemen from Cavan and Monaghan to bring in his harvest at much greater cost.

The Mayo Land League grew into the National Land League, with Charles Stewart Parnell as President and Davitt as Secretary. Their agitation throughout the country was so successful that Prime Minister Gladstone acceded to their demands in the Land Act of 1880, granting tenants fairer rents and fixity of tenure. In 1882, Davitt was elected Member of Parliament but was disqualified because of his earlier conviction for treason on account of his Fenian activities. For the rest of his life, he worked as a freelance journalist, travelling all over the world writing and lecturing. His will, written in 1904, was most specific:

"Should I die in Ireland I would like to be buried at Straide, County Mayo, without any funeral demonstration. If I die in America I must be buried in my mother's grave at Manayunk, near Philadelphia, and on no account be brought back to Ireland, if in any other country (outside of Great Britain) to be buried in the nearest cemetery where I may die, with the simplest possible ceremony . . . My diaries are not to be published without my wife's permission. On no account must anything harsh or censorious, written in said diaries by me about any person dead or alive, who has ever worked for Ireland, be printed, published, or used so as to give pain to any friend or relative. To all my friends I leave kind thoughts; to my enemies the fullest forgiveness; and to Ireland the undying prayer for the absolute freedom and independence which it was my life's ambition to try and obtain for her."

Davitt died in Dublin of acute septic poisoning of the jaw after he had had two teeth extractions. He is buried in Straide graveyard near the old penal chapel where he was baptised, a stone's throw from the site of the home from which he had been evicted.

Buried under the floor of the ruins of the thirteenth century abbey is **Anne Deane** (1828–1905), President of the Ladies' Land League which had been founded by Anna Parnell, Parnell's sister, "to undertake the relief of evicted tenants after the suspension of the habeas corpus Act." The Ladies' League was eventually suppressed by Charles Stewart Parnell who found it too militant. Anne Deane's memorial was erected by her cousin, John Dillon (1851–1927), MP for East Mayo, a prominent agitator for land reform and fair rents who, after the death of John Redmond, became the leader of the Nationalist party. (Beneath Anne Deane's memorial plaque, there is an ancient tomb with unusual medieval carvings of smiling figures, of the Three Wise Men, of St Peter and St Paul, of Christ displaying his five wounds, of a bishop and others, all happily grinning.)

There is now a small museum next to the cemetery grounds with exhibits and papers related to Michael Davitt and the Land League.

KILCONDUFF

Another later agitator for reform, the socialist writer, **Peadar O'Donnell** (1893–1986), is buried in Mayo, in

Kilconduff cemetery, near Swinford. As a teacher on Aranmore, County Donegal, he had been angered by the numbers of his pupils who had to leave school for labouring jobs in Scotland and wrote frequently about the atrocious working and living conditions that they had to endure. When the Achill Island boys lost their lives in the bothy, he angrily wrote how "they were roasted into the headlines." O'Donnell wrote seven novels, including *Islanders* (1927) and founded and edited the influential literary magazine, *The Bell*, with Sean Ó Faolain. He is buried with his partner, Lile, in the O'Donnell tomb, their names written on the back wall of the little structure. (This part of the churchyard was extremely overgrown when I visited it and required wading through waist-high thistles and nettles.)

CLARE ISLAND

Grace O'Malley (1530–1600) was a sea-queen, or more to the point, a pirate, and her name Granuaile ranks with those formidable Irish women such as Queen Maeve and Deirdre as an icon of Ireland. She belonged to one of the old Gaelic families who ruled over much of Connemara. She exercised her power by attacking merchant ships on their way to Galway, levying tolls for their safe passage and making off with their cargoes. In that turbulent century that saw the final surrender of the ancient Irish chieftains to English rule, she too submitted to Sir Henry Sidney, Queen Elizabeth's governor, but managed to continue her pillage and piracy anyway. She is buried in the ruined Cistercian Abbey on Clare Island, in Clew Bay, in the tomb next to a slab which shows the O'Malley arms, a rearing stallion, a boar, three bows and arrows and a galley. There are daily boat trips to the island from Louisburgh, during which, with any luck, you will be able to admire the antics of the bottle-nosed dolphins who often follow the boats.

Grace's son **Tibbot na Long Bourke** (1567–1629), or

Theobald of the Ships, is buried in Ballintubber Abbey in an imposing tomb, now in the sacristy. In 1593 Grace O'Malley visited Queen Elizabeth of England, the only Gaelic woman chief to be received at court, to secure the release of her son who had been captured by English forces. Astonishingly all her requests were granted. Tibbot promptly took up arms against his own clansmen and sided with the English. He fought with the English at the Battle of Kinsale in 1600, was knighted first viscount of Mayo, and became the county's MP. He is thought to have been murdered by his brother-in-law. The tomb, with its altar base showing carvings of the twelve apostles, and huge stone canopy above, was badly damaged by Cromwellian soldiers, but is still an impressive example of seventeenth century workmanship.

LOUGH CARRA

The ashes of the novelist and art critic **George Augustus Moore** (1852–1933) are buried in a cairn on Castle Island on the shores of Lough Carra. The inscription reads:

He forsook his family and friends for his art
But because he was faithful to his art
His family and friends reclaimed his ashes for Ireland
Vale.

As a young man Moore lived the bohemian life of an art student in Paris but left when he felt his talents were not great enough. His first novel, *A Modern Lover* (1883), had the distinction of being banned as decadent. He spent most of the rest of his life in London, following with interest the Irish Literary Revival but wanting little to do with the Irish people or their politics. His funeral oration was written but not delivered by George Russell (AE) who wrote of him:

He loved the land even if he did not love the nation. Yet his enmities even made his nation to be as much admired or loved as the praise of its patriots. If his ashes have any sentience they

*will feel at home here, for the colours of Lough Carra remained
in his memory when many of his other affections had passed.*

During the Civil War, Moore's ancestral home, in common
with so many of the country's "Big Houses", was burned
down by the IRA. Its gaunt shell stands on a hill overlooking
the lake. In 1964, the Ballyglass Company of the Old IRA
erected a plaque on Castle Island in partial atonement. It
declares that "this Catholic patriot family is honoured for their
famine relief and their refusal to barter principles for English
gold."

CASTLEBAR

Moore Hall was built in 1792 by the novelist's ancestor,
another George Moore, a wine trader who carried on a
successful business from Alicante in Spain. His son, **John
Moore** (1767–1799), abandoned his studies for the Bar and
joined the Society of United Irishmen. On hearing that
General Humbert had landed in Killala he travelled to Mayo
and joined the French forces in Castlebar. For one brief week
in 1798, John Moore was appointed President of the
Provisional Republic of Connacht, but was captured by the
English and subsequently sentenced to transportation. While
imprisoned in Waterford waiting for the ship to take him to
Australia, he died. He was buried outside Waterford but his
body was later exhumed and re-interred in a plot beside the
1798 memorial on the Mall in Castlebar which describes him
as the "first president of Ireland".

ROSCOMMON

KILRONAN

Turlough Ó Carolan (1670–1738), the blind harper and composer, is buried near Keadue in the ancient cemetery of Kilronan on the shore of Lough Meelagh. Blinded by smallpox at the age of fourteen, he was then apprenticed to a local harper and thereafter spent the remainder of his life as an itinerant musician, visiting the ancestral homes of Irish noblemen, entertaining them and composing airs to his patrons in return for their hospitality. His wake at Kilronan lasted for four days with thousands of mourners attending from all over Ireland. Many of his compositions were saved and recorded by the antiquarian and musician Edward Bunting. There is a further memorial to him in St Patrick's Cathedral in Dublin. An annual harp festival is held every August in Keadue with musicians, national and international, coming to pay tribute to him.

FRENCHPARK

Douglas Hyde (1860–1949), the poet, scholar, and first president of Ireland, is buried at the old rectory at Frenchpark. Devoted to the collection of folklore and the revival of the Irish language, he was a founder member and first president of the Gaelic League which was to become so influential in the renewal of nationalism at the turn of the century. Hyde felt that for the world to see Ireland as a separate nation with its own culture, the Irish must be "de-Anglicised", must adopt their own language, literature, music, sports and ideas. Although he insisted that the Gaelic League should remain non-political, it caught the popular imagination in a way that made its politicisation inevitable. Hyde resigned the presidency of the League in 1915 and played no part in the political struggles of the period. In 1937 with the adoption of the new constitution, he was unanimously selected as President of Ireland and remained in that position until his death.

TRINITY ISLAND

Douglas Hyde, in his *Love Songs of Connacht,* made a translation of **"Una Bhán"**, one of the most popular and most plaintive Irish love songs. Trinity Island, on Lough Key, is the alleged burial place of the eponymous Una Bhán, daughter of the Chief of the MacDermotts, and her lover, the poet, **Tomás Láidir Costello**. Dismayed by this unsuitable alliance, her father had hastily arranged for Una to be married off to a man of more suitable rank, but to the consternation of the assembly at the wedding feast, Una, when asked to drink a toast to the person she loved, recklessly raised her glass to Tomás. He was promptly expelled from the party. As heroines were then inclined to do, Una fell into a decline from which she could not be saved unless, said her doctors, she was allowed to see Tomás again. When it appeared she was at death's door, her lover was reluctantly summoned. Una rallied and fell into a peaceful sleep. Tomás, now aggrieved by the coolness of his reception by her family, rowed back to the mainland, swearing that he would never return unless he was sent for before he reached dry land. Una, on waking, demanded that a horseman ride after him and recall him but it was too late. Una relapsed and died. When the news of her death reached Tomás he dashed to her grave and sang his heart out:

Oh fair Una, thou has left me in grief twisted . . . And sure I would rather be sleeping in death beside you than to be in the glory of heaven . . .

It was not long before he too pined away and was buried beside her. In the best romantic tradition, two shoots sprang up from the graves and began to grow towards one another until their branches were completely entwined, united only in death. Needless to say, no sign of their graves remain but the lovers still live on in one of the most haunting of Irish laments.

RATHCROGHAN

The legendary ancient queens of the Tuatha de Danann, **Eire**, **Fodhla and Banba**, who gave their names to Ireland, are buried together in the Cemetery of the Kings, six miles south-east of Frenchpark on the hill of Rathcroghan. This area was once the royal capital where the kings of Connacht were inaugurated and it is still studded with many old raths and tumuli. Among them is a seven foot standing stone, a pillar of red sandstone, which is said to mark the grave of **Dathi**, the last pagan monarch of Ireland, who was allegedly killed by a bolt of lightning.

SLIGO

The legendary **Queen Maeve** of Connacht is traditionally thought to be buried in a passage-grave on the top of Knocknarea mountain, five miles west of Sligo. About 200 feet in diameter and thirty-four feet high, the cairn dominates the entire landscape for miles around. It takes about an hour to climb the mountain starting on a sign-posted path about two and a half miles west of Carrowmore.

Maeve was one of those strong, ruthless heroines, part queen, part goddess, written about in the cycle of epic tales in our earliest surviving manuscripts. She was married to **Ailill**. One night, lying on the pillows of their royal bed, they began to argue about which of them was the wealthier. They measured and matched and weighed and counted their property, from jewellery to precious cloth, from rams and horses to cows. In every department they were equal, except that Ailill had one great white-horned bull better than any of Maeve's.

There was, however, a massive brown-horned bull to equal it in Ulster. Maeve and Ailill assembled a huge army from Connacht and joined forces with their allies in the other provinces to invade Ulster to capture the bull. This set in chain a course of events that led to the slaughter of thousands of warriors, including the mighty Cuchulainn, and a pyrrhic victory for the bull of Ulster.

Although tradition has it that Queen Maeve stands within

her tomb on the top of the mountain, sword in hand, wearing full battle-dress and looking towards Ulster from where her enemies might appear, the grave is too ancient to be hers but is simply part of the whole complex of megalithic graves associated with nearby Carrowmore. Ailill, her husband, is supposed to be buried under the cairn situated incongruously behind the garden of a bungalow in the aptly named village of Heapstown, near the shores of Lough Arrow.

CARROWMORE

Carrowmore in the very suburbs of Sligo town is the largest megalithic cemetery in Ireland and the area has been under excavation since the 1970s. The oldest tomb has been dated to about 4,200 BC. There are still about forty passage-tombs, some topped by cairns and dolmens. Carrowmore was an ancient sacred ground – there is no evidence of settlement. Recent excavations have revealed traces of megalithic art, circles and carvings similar to ones found in Brittany. The Stone Age tombs were for cremated remains buried about a metre under the dolmen but the same graves were re-used by Iron and Bronze age dwellers – these are inhumations rather than cremations. Later remains include many cranial parts, perhaps associated with a Celtic cult – early Romans reported that the Celts went into battle wearing nothing but blue body paint and belts of skulls. Finds in these impressive tombs have also included flint arrow-heads, antler pins, ivory bracelets, shards of pottery and stone beads. There is a small admission charge to the explanatory slide display. The site is well sign-posted.

Sligo presents us with more evidence of early man in the spectacular hill-top Carrowkeel Passage Tombs cemetery in the Bricklieve Mountains north of Ballinafad, overlooking Lough Arrow. Here there are the remains of fourteen neolithic passage graves, conical mounds of stone covering a passage-grave, built by Stone Age farmers 5,000 years ago. At the crossroads of Castlebaldwin, follow the signposts for Carrowkeel. The road soon becomes a track, narrowing to a stony path with grass growing up the centre. You can drive up almost all the way, then take a not very strenuous climb to the top of the hill where you are rewarded by stunning views of Lough Arrow and a remote and wild landscape dotted with these extraordinary cairns. One of these is similar to Newgrange in County Meath, though on a lesser scale, and the burial chamber is lit by the sun, not on the winter solstice as in Newgrange but on the summer solstice on 21 June. There are remnants of Stone Age huts on the ridges nearby.

BALLINDOON

Terence MacDonagh, The Counsellor (1640–1713), was the only Catholic in penal times to attend the Irish Bar. His gravestone is under the tower of the ruined abbey on the shores of Lough Arrow. The unusual inscription reads

Terence mac Donnogh lyes wth in this grave
That says enogh for all that's generous, brave,
Fasecious, friendly, witty, Just and Good
And in this lov'd name is fully understood
For it includes whate'er wee Virtue call
And is the hieroglyphick of them all.

Terence MacDonagh belonged to one of the great Gaelic families who ruled the area before the Cromwellian plantations in the seventeenth century who managed to hold on to part of their lands. It was the MacDonaghs who had founded the Abbey of Ballindoon and there are many other family tombstones in this beautiful but rather neglected spot.

DRUMCLIFFE

About four miles north of Sligo, in Drumcliffe graveyard, under the shadow of Ben Bulben, lies one of the giants of Irish literature, the poet **William Butler Yeats** (1865–1939).

The stone, inscribed as he had wished on "limestone quarried near the spot" reads:

> *Cast a cold eye*
> *On Life, on death*
> *Horseman, pass by.*

Yeats had died in Roquebrune near Monaco in 1939, but it was not until 1948 that his remains were brought back from France by Sean MacBride, the son of Maud Gonne, for reburial in Ireland. Yeats' wife, George Hyde-Lees, is buried with him. Inside the church is a memorial to his great-grandfather, John, who was rector of the parish. Be warned that in the summer months the church and graveyard are thronged with hordes of camera-toting tourists.

SLIGO

In a corner of Sligo's main graveyard it is surprising to come up against a monument to "the brave avenger of President Lincoln", **Captain Edward P Doherty** (1809–1865), and to discover that he was the man who captured John Wilkes Booth, the assassin of Abraham Lincoln. In the aftermath of Lincoln's murder in the Ford Theatre in Washington, 10,000 soldiers took part in the hunt for Booth. Doherty, a native of Sligo, was in command of the cavalry patrol that surrounded the isolated barn where the assassin and his accomplice had taken refuge. The barn was set alight and in the ensuing confusion shots rang out. The enquiry that followed never properly established if Booth had been shot or had taken his own life, but Doherty, who had pulled the dying Booth from the blaze, is credited with his capture.

SKREEN

"Souperism" was the loaded epithet used to describe the practice of "bribing" poor Catholics to convert to Protestantism in exchange for food during the mid-nineteenth century famines. One of the most controversial characters associated with this period was the **Reverend Edward Nangle** (1799–1883). He is buried in Skreen graveyard on the road between Sligo and Ballina.

Nangle had visited Achill in 1831 to report on conditions on the island and subsequently returned there to set up a proselytising missionary colony. Driven equally by the desire to minister to the islanders' spiritual and physical needs, he founded a school, church, hospital, orphanage and printing press in Dugort and set about introducing new land reclamation schemes. Unfortunately, his religious beliefs were expressed in violent anti-Catholicism in an outpouring of pamphlets and editorials from his printing press and in his newpaper *The Achill Missionary Herald,* so bringing him into hostile opposition with the Catholic Archbishop of Tuam, **John McHale** (1791–1881), himself a controversial figure. In particular, the archbishop opposed the introduction of compulsory national schooling at the time because of his fears of proselytising. These two strong-willed men fought out the battle for the souls of the Achill islanders against the tragic background of the famine.

There is no doubt that Nangle did much to alleviate poverty, made endless petitions on the island's behalf and created much needed employment. In the end, the barrenness of the land, the prevalence of disease and relentless famine all defeated him. He left Achill after the worst famine years and became rector of Skreen from 1852–1873. His adversary, Archbishop John McHale, is buried in St Jarlath's Cathedral, Tuam, County Galway.

LEINSTER

CARLOW

TULLOW

> *At Vinegar Hill, o'er the pleasant Slaney*
> *Our heroes vainly stood back to back,*
> *And the yeos at Tullow took Father Murphy*
> *and burnt his body upon the rack.*
>
> *(Traditional air)*

After the defeat of the United Irishmen at the battle of Vinegar Hill in Wexford, **Father John Murphy** (1753–1798), became a fugitive. He and a comrade, James Gallagher, eventually arrived in Tullow on 3 July 1798 where they were captured by yeomen and handed over to the authorities for interrogation. His interrogators may not even have known his true identity for there had been rumours that the priest had been slain in battle. Both men were publicly flogged in the market square, hanged and decapitated. Father Murphy's headless body was then dumped into a barrel of pitch and set alight. What remained of his body was later rescued and taken clandestinely for burial at the Mullawn, the cemetery on the outskirts of the town of Tullow. The precise location of the grave is unknown. A monument to Father Murphy of Boolavogue and James Gallagher stands in Tullow Square at the site of their execution.

GRAIGUE

The cruelty of death by slow hanging only came to an end

with the invention of the "long drop", a system of hanging invented by a Carlow-born scientist, the Reverend Samuel Haughton (1821–1897). Professor Haughton's motives were entirely humanitarian. Until the introduction of the Haughton system, hanging was a slow and cruel death by strangulation and it is quite likely that hanged men were still alive when taken down for drawing, that is, disembowelling, and quartering. Haughton's system was based on a precise mathematical formula which calculated the length of the "drop" needed in proportion to the weight of the person to be hanged. Horrendous as it seems to us now, it had the advantage of procuring a rapid death by severing the spinal cord. Haughton was one of those versatile Victorians, mineralogist, marine scientist, zoologist, campaigning doctor during Dublin's cholera epidemic and a prominent member of the Gaelic League at Trinity College. He died in Dublin where a huge number of academics, clerics, students and notables attended his funeral; his remains were then taken for burial in the family plot at Killeshin Church, about half a mile out of Graigue on the N80 towards Portlaoise. (Confusingly there is a small village of Killeshin in the same area where I spent a fruitless hour hunting for Haughton's grave. It is well worth the detour, however, as its ruined church has a magnificent Romanesque doorway.)

BORRIS

Arthur MacMurrough Kavanagh (1831–1889) overcame severe handicaps to become a distinguished landlord, sportsman and MP. Despite being born with only the most rudimentary arms and legs, true to his background, he rode to hounds, learned to shoot, fish, sail and ride a horse. When he was only twenty-two years of age he inherited the family estates at Borris and proved to be a most generous and responsible landlord. He rebuilt the village of Borris which had suffered greatly in the famine years and had a Catholic chapel built in the workhouse, the first workhouse in the country to have one. He also served for many years as an MP for Wexford and for Carlow. He died on Christmas Day 1889, aged fifty-eight, and was buried in the private graveyard on the demesne at Borris House, Borris, near Muine Beag (Bagenalstown). The gravestone is a large Celtic cross with an inscription from Matthew: "His Lord said unto him Well done thou good and faithful servant, Thou hast been faithful over a few things. I will make thee ruler over many things. Enter thou into the joy of the Lord." There is also a monument in his memory in St Canice's Cathedral, Kilkenny, inscribed to Art MacMurrough Kavanagh "who rendered services to the church in the sorest hour of her need."

St Mullins

In the graveyard of the church in St Mullins there are the remains of a monastery founded in the seventh century, once the most important religious site in the county and the former burial place of the kings of Leinster before Ferns in Wexford became dominant. The Gaelic king, **Art MacMurrough** (d.1417), is buried here. In the last quarter of the fourteenth century Art MacMurrough led the resistance to Anglo-Norman rule in Ireland from his stronghold in the Barrow valley, exacting tribute and controlling the main access routes between Dublin and the Norman towns of Kilkenny, Waterford and Wexford. In 1399 he fought against Richard II, the last English king in the middle ages to come in person to wage war in Ireland and force the Gaelic chieftains to surrender to the crown. It was a disastrous engagement for the Plantagenet army who were totally at a loss in the hostile terrain of river, forest and marsh, and ran out of food. Richard eventually had to leave without resolving the Irish question when Henry Bolingbroke, back in England, seized his throne, becoming Henry IV. For the time being Gaelic Ireland was left to its own devices.

The grave of one of the prominent figures of the 1798 rebellion and one of the few to have lived to see old age is also here in St Mullins. **General Thomas Cloney** (1774–1850), fought with Father Murphy at Vinegar Hill and at Wexford town. Imprisoned and condemned to death, he was reprieved after two years in prison and exiled from Ireland. He returned in 1803 and took part in Robert Emmet's rising. He subsequently came to live in Graiguenamanagh where he remained active politically in the campaign for Catholic emancipation and for the repeal of the Union. He developed a close relationship with Daniel O'Connell who, at his request, held one of his monster rallies at Graiguenamanagh. Until the end of his life, he was held in high regard as "the old general of '98".

BROWNE'S HILL, NEAR CARLOW

Dotted around the county there are many ancient pre-historic sites, ring-forts, cashels and dolmens. The most striking of these is the Browne's Hill dolmen, a few miles outside Carlow on the road to Tullow. This was a neolithic burial ground and the dolmen has been standing in this field for over 5,000 years. Its claim to fame is that it has the largest capstone in Europe, an enormous structure resting on two portal stones. There is free public access to view it by a path which is clearly signposted.

DUBLIN

After the Reformation, all Catholic burials in Dublin had to take place in the churchyards of the established church. In 1823, a well-respected citizen, Arthur D'Arcy, was being buried in St Kevin's in Camden Row when the Protestant archbishop, Dr Magee, forbade the priest, Dr Blake, to say the Prayers for the Deceased over the grave. The indignant mourners were on the brink of rioting but Dr Blake managed to defuse the situation by asking them to join together in silent prayer. The incident proved to be a turning-point. It prompted the formation of a committee of the Catholic Association, chaired by the lawyer Daniel O'Connell, to look into the whole issue of Catholic burials.

The crux of the matter was the law that forbade Catholics to purchase property. O'Connell successfully challenged this and, eventually, in 1828, a site was bought at Golden Bridge in Inchicore for the sum of £600 where Catholics could bury their dead "free of harassment". A second plot was later acquired on the north side of the Liffey. At first called Prospect, it is more usually known as Glasnevin Cemetery.

Today Glasnevin is one of Dublin's largest cemeteries and is non-denominational. Surrounded by high walls topped with towers from where the night-watchmen once kept a look out for "sack-em-ups" bent on snatching fresh corpses for sale to surgeons, the cemetery is now dominated by the round tower

45

which stands over the crypt where "old Dan O'" himself is buried.

Daniel O'Connell (1775–1847), known as The Liberator, was the lawyer who mobilised the movement for Catholic emancipation, not by the use of violence, but by bringing issue after issue to law, and organising monster rallies all over the country. Although Catholics were not entitled to sit in parliament, O'Connell saw there was no law preventing a Catholic going forward as a candidate. He stood in Clare in 1828 and was elected by a large majority. This led directly to the passing of the Catholic Emancipation Act in 1829, making O'Connell the undisputed hero of the Irish people.

In 1847, as the famine worsened in Ireland, he made a last trip to Westminster to appeal for more relief from a parliament where, he wrote, "there seems to be an ignorance of the real state of horror in which Ireland is plunged." He was already very ill and, persuaded by doctors to go to a warmer climate, set off on a nightmarish journey to Rome with his friend and priest, Dr Miley, his son and a manservant. His condition rapidly deteriorated. He was in turns depressed and agitated, never letting the priest out of his sight, night or day, and finally died in Genoa in Italy. At his request, though it seems a strange one for a man who had devoted his life to Ireland, his heart was encased in a silver urn and sent to Rome. The remains of his body were returned to Ireland for burial.

Another colossus of Irish history, **Charles Stewart Parnell** (1846–1891), is buried in a large round railed-in area to the left of the O'Connell tower. An enormous boulder of Wicklow granite, brought from the Parnell estate, and simply inscribed "Parnell", stands over his grave. Parnell, "the uncrowned king of Ireland", was the Protestant landowner who almost achieved Home Rule for Ireland. His Irish party had won a massive majority in the 1885 elections, and Prime Minister Gladstone, needing the support of Parnell and his party in a hung parliament, reversed his opposition to Home

Rule. Unfortunately, in 1890, Parnell was named as co-respondent in the divorce of Captain William O'Shea – his wife, Kitty, had been Parnell's mistress for years. The Catholic Church mounted a vitriolic campaign against him, dividing the country into Parnellites and anti-Parnellites. Parnell was toppled from the leadership of his party. He died the following year in Brighton, by then having married Mrs O'Shea in Steyning registry office. Maud Gonne brought his body back to Ireland. His funeral in Glasnevin was attended by thousands. Among the mourners was WB Yeats who noted the number of wreaths with the angry inscription "Murdered by the priests".

This part of the cemetery is the site of many unmarked graves, the destitute victims of the cholera epidemics which raged through the country in the 1830s and 1840s.

Opposite the main gate into the cemetery is the grave of **Sir Roger Casement** (1864–1916). Casement was executed for treason at Pentonville prison in August 1916, a few months after the other leaders of the 1916 Rising were executed at Kilmainham Gaol. He had been arrested in April after he had landed at Banna Strand with a German ship, the *Aud*, trying to smuggle in a consignment of arms from Germany for use in the Rising. An unlikely recruit to the cause of Irish nationalism, Casement had worked in the British colonial service where he had reported on the mistreatment of black workers in the Belgian Congo and the cruel treatment of native Indians by white traders in Peru. After his arrest and execution, diaries, alleged to be his and including references to his homosexuality, were circulated by the British. For some time these were thought to be a slanderous forgery but are now believed to be authentic, though one can hardly applaud the government's motives in releasing them. Casement's remains were returned for re-interment in March 1965 when he was given a state funeral. Non-Irish speakers note that the gravestone is inscribed: "Ruairi MacEasmainn".

A simple granite plinth inscribed "The Labour Leader" marks the grave of **James Larkin** (1876–1947), the founder of the Irish Transport and General Workers' Union in 1909. A powerful orator, he moved the rights of workers on to the political agenda, but the bitter, and sometimes violent, industrial disputes led to the Dublin lock-out in 1913/14. Subsequently he went to America where he was imprisoned for his activities on behalf of the Wobblies, the International Workers of the World, so was absent during the 1916 Rising and the War of Independence.

Opposite Larkin is the grave of **Maud Gonne MacBride** (1866–1953). She was the fiercely republican muse of William Butler Yeats and the object of his passionate though unrequited love. Her performance in the role of Cathleen ní Houlihan in Yeats' play in 1902 was so stirring (Cathleen ní Houlihan being the embodiment of Ireland, an old hag transformed into a radiant queen by the martyrdom of young men prepared to lay down their lives for her) that Yeats later asked if "that play of mine sent out/Certain men the English shot?"

She is buried with her son, the politician, diplomat and recipient of the Nobel Peace Prize, **Sean MacBride**, (1904–1989).

Nearby is **Jeremiah O'Donovan Rossa** (1831–1915), a member of the revolutionary Irish Republican Brotherhood, the secret society established simultaneously in New York and Dublin to fight for Irish independence in the post-famine years.

O'Donovan Rossa had lived with relatives in Skibbereen, one of the areas worst affected by the famine. After his father died and the family had been evicted from their home, he saw at first hand the devastating suffering of the time. After the famine years, O'Donovan Rossa was one of the founders of the Phoenix Society of Skibbereen, a forerunner of the Fenian movement. The Fenians were fiercely nationalistic, disposed to armed rebellion and able to draw support from the huge numbers of Irish who had emigrated from Ireland as a result of the famine. O'Donovan Rossa was eventually imprisoned in England and his account of his imprisonment is told in his *Jail Journal* (1874). He was released in bad health on condition that he did not return to Ireland.

After his death in the United States in 1915, his remains were returned for burial in Dublin where his funeral proved to be a huge rallying-point for nationalists. The funeral oration was given by Patrick Pearse:

"They think that they have foreseen everything; they think they have provided against everything; but the fools, the fools, they have left us our Fenian dead and while Ireland holds these graves, Ireland unfree shall never be at peace."

Nearby in the Republican plot are many of these graves. **John O'Leary** (1830–1907), another Fenian leader, was editor of the *Irish People*. An excerpt from the speech he made in 1903 on the centenary of Emmet's death is inscribed on the cross: "Emmet desired that his epitaph should not be written until his country was free: strive with might and main to bring about the hour when his epitaph can be written. I have nothing more to say, but I and all of you have very much to do."

In his later life, O'Leary became the mentor of both Yeats and Maud Gonne. Yeats' poem, September 1913, laments that

Romantic Ireland's dead and gone
It's with O'Leary in the grave."

In fact **James Stephens** (1825–1901) is, if not with, at least beside O'Leary in the grave under the inscription "A day, an hour, of virtuous liberty is worth a whole eternity in bondage."

Stephens was the founder, organizer and chief of the Irish Fenian Brotherhood and distinguishes himself from all the other dead around him in that he had two funerals, more than fifty years apart. When he was on the run in 1848 after the disastrous and short-lived rebellion at Ballingarry, his friends placed a death notice in the Kilkenny newspapers and held a huge mock funeral, the coffin packed with boulders. Meanwhile Stephens sailed from Cork to Paris, disguised as a ladies' maid. Years later, after another aborted uprising which had to be abandoned when promised arms failed to materialise, he was arrested again and once again managed to escape, this time from the Richmond Prison. By then he was out of favour with the American Fenians and dropped out of political life. (This James Stephens is not of course James Stephens (1880–1950) the diminutive poet, friend of James Joyce and author of *The Crock of Gold* who is buried in London.)

Countess Constance Markievicz (1868–1927), the rebel countess, Irish republican and champion of women's rights is also buried in the Republican plot. This extraordinary Irish beauty, wife of a Polish count she had married in Paris, had become involved with the Gaelic League in 1908, joined Sinn Féin and ran soup kitchens during the Dublin lock-out. She was condemned to death for her part in the 1916 Rising but the sentence was later commuted to penal servitude. She spent periods on the run, on hunger strike and in jail. Markievicz was the first woman to be elected to the British Parliament but, in line with Sinn Féin policy, did not take her seat, instead becoming a member of the First Dáil and Minister for Labour, making her the first woman in modern history to hold ministerial office.

Robert Erskine Childers (1870–1922), also seems to be an unlikely recruit to the Republican cause. An Anglo-Irishman who had been a clerk in the House of Commons, he worked for British intelligence and fought in the Boer War. He was the author of the novel, *The Riddle of the Sands,* a remarkable spy story about two yachtsmen who discover the Germans are preparing to invade England. It has never been out of print since it was published in 1903.

Later, Childers became a passionate advocate of Irish nationalism, joined Sinn Féin, and, in 1914, ran a consignment of German rifles for the Irish Volunteers into Howth in his own yacht, the *Asgard*, a wedding present from his father-in-law. (The yacht, incidentally, can be seen in Kilmainham Jail.) In the Civil War that followed the signing of the Anglo-Irish Treaty, Childers was arrested and executed by firing squad by the Irish Free State government in 1922. First buried at Beggar's Bush, he was re-interred in Glasnevin two years later.

Eamon de Valera (1882–1975) was, for decades, one of the dominant figures of Irish political life. He was court-martialled for his part in the 1916 Rising but his death sentence was commuted to life imprisonment and he was released the following year. Imprisoned again in 1918, he was "sprung" from Lincoln Jail by Michael Collins and unanimously elected Príomh Aire of the newly-proclaimed Irish Republic. He then embarked on a mission to the United States to win official recognition of the Republic and, while that objective was not reached, his visit raised millions of dollars in republican "bonds".

Following the negotiations with the British government to put an end to the War of Independence, de Valera opposed the Anglo-Irish treaty since it granted only limited autonomy to twenty-six counties and required an oath of allegiance to the king. The treaty was debated by Dáil Éireann where de Valera declared: " . . . (the treaty) will not end the centuries of conflict between the two nations . . . the Irish people would not want me to save them materially at the expense of their national honour . . . "

The treaty was accepted by a majority of sixty-four to fifty-seven but de Valera withdrew his supporters and refused to accept the validity of the vote. The foundation of the new Irish state was immediately marred by the outbreak of civil war.

In April 1926 de Valera founded Fianna Fáil. He went on to hold office as Taoiseach in several Fianna Fáil governments, and later as President of Ireland for two terms. He was also the architect of the 1937 constitution. He is buried in a surprisingly modest grave next to his wife **Sinéad de Valera** (1878–1975), a children's writer and compiler of Irish legends.

A limestone cross marks the grave of "The Big Fellow" **Michael Collins** (1890–1922), which is to the right of the main entrance gate, near the wall, and in the centre of a plot commemorating many of those killed during the Civil War.

With Arthur Griffith, Collins had taken part in the negotiations which led to the signing of the Anglo-Irish treaty in December 1921. At the treaty debates the following month, he argued for its acceptance, declaring that "it gives us freedom, not the ultimate freedom that all nations desire and develop to, but freedom to achieve it."

Collins became Commander-in-Chief of the government forces, even procuring arms from Churchill, colonial secretary at the time, to help recapture the Four Courts, the seizure of which by the anti-treaty republicans had marked the start of the Civil War. He was killed in an ambush at Béal na Bláth in County Cork. His remains were brought back to Dublin by ship for a state funeral. After his body was embalmed by the writer-surgeon, Oliver St John Gogarty, Collins was painted by the artist Sir John Lavery, with whose wife, Hazel, Collins may, or may not, have had an affair. Contemporary newspapers show the streets of Dublin lined with thousands of flag-waving mourners as his coffin was escorted in a gun-carriage led by four black horses to Glasnevin for a state funeral. The Civil War dragged on until the following May 1923.

The founder of Sinn Féin, **Arthur Griffith** (1871–1922), and Collins' colleague in the negotiation of the treaty, is also buried here in Glasnevin. Griffith was de facto head of the

Irish government in 1919–20 when de Valera was in America. He was responsible for the policy of civil resistance to British rule and the setting up of Sinn Féin courts while Michael Collins led the campaign of guerilla warfare and intelligence gathering. He was elected president after de Valera's withdrawal from the Dáil when the treaty was accepted but died suddenly of a heart attack in August 1922, ten days before Michael Collins was killed.

Brendan Behan, (1923–1964), the colourful Dublin playwright, was buried here in Glasnevin with an IRA guard of honour. His play, *The Quare Fellow,* (1954) was based on life in an Irish prison – Behan served six years of a twelve year sentence for shooting at a policeman, coincidentally in Glasnevin after a republican funeral. Some of the years he spent in prison were in the Curragh with other IRA men such as Máirtín Ó Cadhain (see Mount Jerome) who were interned there for the duration of the Second World War during which time he learned Irish and began to write. He was released under a general amnesty in 1946.

The Quare Fellow was first produced to great success in Ireland but it was Joan Littlewood's production in the Stratford Theatre in London that really launched Behan's international career, even though it was felt in some quarters that she had made it incomprehensible under a blanket of "stage Oirishry".

Behan's step-uncle, **Peadar Kearney** (1883–1942), wrote the words of what is now the Irish national anthem, "The Soldier's Song", as early as 1907 when it was popular as a rallying song. Although it was often sung in the internment camps after the 1916 Rising, it was not officially adopted as the National Anthem until the Dublin Horse Show of 1926 when, for the first time, the Irish tricolor flag flew over the Governor General's Box and "The Soldier's Song" was played. Neither Kearney nor Patrick Heeney (the composer of the music – see Drumcondra) had ever been officially compensated by the state for adopting the music and the title and it was not until 1933 that Kearney was eventually paid a royalty of £1000. He is buried in the republican plot near John O'Leary.

Anne Devlin (1778–1851), is buried at the end of an avenue (site BC43, South) to the right of the O' Connell tower. The niece of the 1798 leader, Michael Dwyer of Wicklow, and the devoted servant of Robert Emmet, she was imprisoned after the failure of Emmet's rebellion in 1803. For two years, she was cruelly mistreated and tortured by Dr Trevor, the superintendent of the jail. After her release, she spent the rest of her life in great hardship and poverty. Shortly before her death, she was discovered and assisted by Dr RR Madden, the historian of the United Irishmen, and it was he who erected the headstone over her grave.

As it had become almost illegible, the original was replaced by the Dublin Cemeteries Committee in 1904. It carries the same inscription: "To the memory of Anne Devlin (Campbell) the faithful servant of Robert Emmett (sic) who possessed some rare and many noble qualities, who lived in obscurity and poverty and so died on the eighteenth day of September 1851 aged 70 years."

The brilliant but doomed poet, **James Clarence Mangan** (1803–1849), author of *My Dark Rosaleen,* died in Dublin destitute, malnourished and addicted to opium. Although not formally educated, Mangan mastered languages and worked for a while in Trinity College Library and on the Ordnance Survey with the antiquarian George Petrie. However, his addictions to alcohol and opium destroyed him. When he collapsed in a Dublin street with nothing but a few coins in his pocket and a book of German poetry, he looked like a skeleton. He died in the Meath Hospital. James Joyce once described him as "the most significant poet of the modern Celtic world". His work, still neglected, seems a precursor of Yeats. There is another memorial to Mangan in St Stephen's

Green in Dublin. It is a bust of the poet by the sculptor Oliver Sheppard with a marble representation in a niche underneath of "My Dark Rosaleen" by the stone-mason Willie Pearse, brother of Patrick Pearse.

It is now thought that Mangan may have died of cholera for Dublin that year was swept by a great epidemic which had been spreading across Asia and Europe since 1845. Over 11,000 victims of cholera were buried in Glasnevin in 1849 alone. Mangan is buried in Dublin Section five.

A near contemporary of Mangan, **Michael Moran** (1794–1846), was a well-known eccentric and itinerant story-teller, better known as Zozimus. He had become blind shortly after his birth but went on to become a famous, if bad-tempered, personality as he wandered around the city dressed in distinctive scalloped cape, wielding a blackthorn stick tied to his wrist with a strip of leather and reciting his rhymes and stories to large crowds with frequent abusive asides about their stinginess.

He had adopted the name Zozimus from a legend about an Egyptian cleric who found Mary living as a hermit in the desert and one of his most popular recitations was about their encounter. Zozimus's ballads, like "St Patrick Was A Gintilman", may still be heard in Dublin pubs. His grave is in the paupers' plot near the Parnell enclosure.

Patrick Weston Joyce (1827–1914), was an influential figure in the Gaelic Revival. President of the Royal Society of Antiquaries of Ireland, and principal of a Dublin teacher training college, he was the author of *The Origin and History of Irish Names of Places* (1870) and *A Social History of Ancient Ireland* (1903). He was also an enthusiastic collector of traditional Irish airs and songs, published as Old Irish Folk Music and Songs, and adjudicated at the first Oireachtas organised by the Gaelic League.

Another musician and composer who did much to revive interest in traditional music was the German **Carl Gilbert Hardebeck** (1869–1945), who is buried here with an attractive headstone with an engraving of a harp and the words "He made our old songs live again" inscribed in both English and Irish.

Not far away, in the St Brigid's section, is the lexicographer, **Father Patrick Dineen**, or Pádraig O'Duinnín (1860–1934), another active member of the Gaelic League. Dineen had been a Jesuit priest but left the order after some disagreement and thereafter made his living by freelance writing and compiling an Irish-English dictionary which is still very much in use. Writers will sympathise with his remark in the preface to his dictionary that he had spent twenty years of severe labour "led by the lure and prompted by the pathos of unfinished or undeveloped undertakings."

Another Jesuit, the poet and scholar **Gerard Manley Hopkins** (1844–1889), lies in the communal plot of the Jesuit Order. (The precise location of his grave is unmarked.) A late convert to Catholicism, Hopkins had been sent to University College Dublin as professor of Latin and Greek, spent five unhappy and depressed years there and died of typhoid fever.

Further down this avenue is the grave of **Sean T Ó Ceallaigh** (1882–1966), President of Ireland from 1945–1959. He had been a founder member of Sinn Féin and of Fianna Fáil. He was captain to Patrick Pearse at the GPO during the 1916 Rising.

A little further down the avenue on the same side is the grave of the writer Patricia Lynch. **Patricia Lynch** (1898–1972), for decades the doyenne of children's writing in Ireland, wrote more than fifty books which went into many editions and translations and were illustrated by artists such as Jack B Yeats and Sean Keating. Few people are aware that she had been active in the movement for female emancipation and was a great friend of Eva Gore Booth and Countess Markievicz. Resident in England in 1916, she was sent by Mrs Pankhurst to report on the Easter Rising for *The Workers'*

Dreadnought, and wrote what is often described as the first sympathetic account to be published in Britain.

After her husband's death she lived in Dublin with the puppet theatre family, the Lamberts, and it was they who erected the stone in her memory. Her husband, **RM Fox** (1891–1969), the socialist author and critic, is buried with her.

The feminist and suffragette, **Hanna Sheehy-Skeffington** (d.1946), is also buried in Glasnevin. In 1908 she co-founded the Irish Women's Franchise League to fight for votes for women and for Home Rule. Both an ardent feminist and nationalist, she was the widow of the pacifist, **Francis Sheehy-Skeffington** (1878–1916), who had adopted her surname on marriage on feminist principles. During the 1916 Rising, he had been taken as a hostage on a raiding expedition by the British Army when he saw his arresting officer, Captain Bowen-Colhurst, shoot an unarmed boy. The following morning, Bowen-Colhurst had Sheehy-Skeffington shot dead. As a result the British officer was court-martialled but was deemed to have been of unsound mind when he made the decision and was allowed to emigrate to Canada a year later. Eventually, Mrs Sheehy-Skeffington was offered compensation for her husband's life but refused to accept it. Hanna is believed to be the model for the character of the keen Gaelic Revivalist, Miss Ivors, in James Joyce's story *The Dead.*

Sir Alfred Chester Beatty (1875–1968), the mining engineer and philanthropist who donated his entire and priceless collection of oriental art and manuscripts to the nation (the museum is in Shrewsbury Road, Ballsbridge), died in Monte Carlo, but is buried here to the right of the main entrance of the cemetery, his grave marked by a large handsome granite stone.

A New Yorker by birth, he was the first person to be made an honorary citizen of Ireland and was granted a state funeral.

Across the road, in the newer St Paul's section of

Glasnevin cemetery, there are a number of other interesting Dubliners, among them, **Christy Brown**, author and artist, whose autobiography *My Left Foot* became a successful Oscar-winning film. He was born into a large family in Crumlin – his mother gave birth to twenty-three children – and despite being completely paralysed except for his left foot, he learned to paint and type. He died in 1981 and is buried with his parents. **Luke Kelly** (d.1984), the much-loved musician with The Dubliners, is also buried here. The epitaph on his grave is most appropriate: it says simply "Dubliner".

On the right hand side of the avenue near the entrance is the grave of another popular hero – it is the grave of one of the "Busby Babes", the twenty-two-year-old **Liam Whelan,** one of the Manchester United football team killed when their plane crashed at Munich airport on 6 February 1958. The team was returning from Belgrade after qualifying for the European Cup semi-finals; seven footballers died as well as eight journalists.

A very useful map of Glasnevin is for sale at the office in the cemetery – though it is not without inaccuracies.

MOUNT JEROME CEMETERY

Dublin's other famous cemetery, Mount Jerome, is on the opposite side of the city in Harold's Cross. Dating from 1836, much of it is extremely overgrown and unkempt and dogged perseverance is required to locate graves among its rampant buddleia bushes, bolting brambles, tangles of ivy and massive yew trees. It is redolent of an Ireland that has gone forever, being the final burial ground for so many loyal servants of the crown such as the royal astronomer **William Rowan Hamilton** (1805–1865). Here too are lord chancellors, admirals, the daughters of bishops and wives of baronets. There are several startlingly ostentatious vaults and plinths, speaking louder than any words of the wealth and status of the deceased. The connoisseur of the late Victorian monument will love the massive anchors, urns, avenging angels and distraught weeping women. It is noticeable too how so few of these Victorians died. Rather they "fell asleep in Jesus", "went to Heaven", "entered into rest", or were "called home suddenly".

If you walk directly up the avenue from the main gate to the church and turn right, you will shortly see a massive plinth, topped with what appears to be a huge stone bath. This is the grave and memorial of **Thomas Drummond** (1797–1840), inventor of the limelight (the theatrical spotlight). Certainly with a memorial of these dimensions, Drummond can have no fear of not being seen.

Although the limelight has come to be associated in most people's minds with the theatre, in fact Drummond was a Scottish engineer who had come up with his invention to solve the problem of carrying out observations for the Ordnance Survey in murky weather or night light. The Drummond light was a sensational success, revolutionised the taking of measurements, and was adopted for use in lighthouses. After his experiences in Ireland on the first Ordnance Survey here, he entered politics and made quite a success at it. From 1835–1840 he was Under-Secretary for Ireland, his rule marked by a greater degree of impartiality than had been the case in the previous years when there were violent disturbances between landlords and tenants in the so-called tithe wars. Drummond memorably warned Irish landlords that "property had its duties as well as its rights" and that neglect of their duties in the past had directly led to the "diseased state of society". His last words are inscribed in the stone :

> *Bury me in Ireland*
> *Land of my adoption*
> *I have loved her well*
> *And served her faithfully.*

To the left of the Drummond monument and down a few paths, you will find the grave of **Thomas Davis** (1814–1845), the Dublin barrister who founded *The Nation,* the newspaper of the Young Ireland movement. The son of a British army surgeon, he sought to define the idea of the Irish nation as including everyone who lived in Ireland, regardless of their creed or perceived origins. In his prose and his ballads, Davis's emphasis on past exploitations and grievances helped stir up a fierce anti-British nationalism. Among the many songs attributed to him are "A Nation Once Again" and "The West's Awake", both wildly popular during his lifetime and still popular in many quarters today.

Like many Irish poets, Davis wrote a poem about how he wanted to be buried. In "My Grave", he speculates whether his corpse would be flung in the battle mound or "on the wild heath where the wilder breath of the storm doth blow". He concluded that he wanted to be *"on an Irish green hill-side/on an opening lawn – but not too wide/for I love the drip of the wetted trees./ On me blow no gales but a gentle breeze/to freshen the turf: put no tombstone there/but green sods deck'd with daisies fair/ Be my epitaph writ on my country's mind/ He serv'd his country and lov'd his kind./Oh! 'twere merry unto the grave to go/If one were sure to be buried so."*

The line "He serv'd his country and lov'd his kind" is written on the tombstone but, regrettably, there are no lawns decked with daisies fair.

The playwright, **JM Synge** (1871–1909), is buried here with other members of his family. It was the controversial reception of his play, *The Playboy of the Western World*, in the Abbey Theatre in 1907 that inspired the famous riots. Molly Allgood (1887–1952), the actress who played the role of Pegeen Mike, was Synge's fiancée, but they never married. Synge died of Hodgkin's disease.

A painting of Molly's sister, the actress Sara Allgood, by Sarah Purser hangs in the foyer of the Abbey Theatre. **Sarah Purser** (1848–1943), was a redoubtable woman. Her gravestone is engraved *Fortis et strenua,* "strong and active", a fitting epitaph to a woman who, in her long life, achieved so much but who, like many women in history, has been largely forgotten.

She was well-known as a portrait painter, including studies of her friends Eva and Constance Gore-Booth, and set up An Túr Gloinne, the stained glass studio. She arranged the first major exhibitions in Dublin of the works of Corot, Degas, Manet and Monet in 1899 and was instrumental in the choice of the Municipal Gallery to house the Hugh Lane collection. She died at an advanced age of a stroke, provoked by an argument she had had with President Douglas Hyde about the design of a new postage stamp commemorating the fiftieth anniversary of the Gaelic League.

The rather better known artist **Jack B Yeats** (1871–1957), brother of WB Yeats, is also buried in Mount Jerome. So too is the poet, painter, mystic and essayist, **George Russell**, (AE), (1867–1935). A great friend of Yeats and mentor to a new generation of Irish writers, AE was a very influential figure in Dublin's literary life, holding court in his home in Rathgar on Sunday evenings. Frank O'Connor wrote an affectionate portrait of him in *The Bell* magazine in 1940. "He was a big man; burly, clumsy, untidy, with wild hair and long brown beard, tufted eyebrows and a broad soft red face with high cheekbones that was very like the famous bust of Socrates". Russell was influential in other fields: he was a pioneer of the cooperative movement and was invited to the United States by President Franklin D Roosevelt to lecture on schemes to combat employment among young people by having them undertake public works.

Other writers buried here include **Sheridan le Fanu** (1814–73), the author of the novel *Uncle Silas*. After his wife's death le Fanu lived in morbid solitude in his house at Merrion Square where he wrote his spine-tingling ghost stories *In A Glass Darkly*, tales of malevolent monkeys and vampirish women.

The novelist **William Carleton** (1794–1869), walked to Dublin from his home in Tyrone at the age of twenty-four, observing that he spotted countless rotting corpses hanging from gibbets as he passed through the countryside. His novels portray a vivid picture of nineteenth century life in Ireland as it had never been described before, containing stories of famine, eviction, squalor and executions. Surprisingly for a man of his background, he opposed Catholic emancipation and later adopted the Protestant faith. Benedict Kiely has written his biography, *Poor Scholar.*

One likes to imagine that the author of *Cré na Cille* (Graveyard Clay), **Máirtín Ó Cadhain**, (1906–1970), is carrying on underground conversations with all his motley companions in Mount Jerome. In his book, the corpses in the graveyard talk to one another, going over old quarrels, picking at old wounds and extracting the latest news from the recently buried. Its cast includes the status-conscious Caitríona who is annoyed to find she has been buried in the fifteen shilling plot instead of the pound plot she had left money to pay for, a man who has died of drink from teaching Irish at the rate of a word for a pint, football fans, schoolteachers, republicans, a Free French pilot and a host of the vain and the greedy. Butting in every so often with orders and irritating speeches is the Voice of Authority, ignored at all times. *Cré na Cille* was translated into several European languages, one of a series of books published by UNESCO to celebrate masterpieces written in minority languages.

Ó Cadhain had been a teacher but was dismissed for his support of the IRA during the 1930s. He was interned in the Curragh during the Second World War where he taught Irish to many of his fellow inmates, including Brendan Behan. In 1969 he was appointed Professor of Irish at Trinity College, Dublin.

ST PATRICK'S CATHEDRAL

The graves of **Jonathan Swift** (1667–1745), and his

beloved *Stella,* **Esther Johnson** (1682–1728), lie beneath the floor of St Patrick's Cathedral at the west end of the nave. On the wall nearby is the marble tablet with the epitaph he wrote for himself in Latin. It has been translated by Yeats:

Swift has sailed into his rest;
Savage Indignation there
cannot lacerate his breast.
Imitate him if you dare
World-besotted traveller, he
Served human liberty.

Swift was born in Dublin, educated at Kilkenny and Trinity College, Dublin, and frequently moved between Ireland and England, accepting the position of Dean of St Patrick's in 1713 when it was clear nothing better would come up in London. He was a savage satirist whose *Modest Proposal For Preventing the Children of Ireland from Being a Burden to their Parents or Country* ("a young healthy child well nursed is at a year old a most nourishing and wholsesome food, whether stewed, roasted, baked, or boiled") is a cold business-like proposition underscoring the contempt and ridicule Swift felt for those who maladministered the affairs of Ireland. He spent vast amounts of his income on charities, leaving money to found St Patrick's Hospital for Imbeciles, reputedly after seeing a group of lunatics forced to beg for their supper. He was himself considered insane towards the end of his life though the illness he suffered is now thought to have been Meniere's Disease. In a poem in which he looked forward to his own death, he wrote:

He gave the little wealth he had
To build a house for fools and mad;
And show'd by one satiric touch,
No nation wanted it so much.

Frederick, Duke Schomberg, commander of the Williamite forces, was killed at the Battle of the Boyne in 1690. The inscription over his tomb was written in Latin by

Dean Swift and indignantly relates how the dean and chapter of the cathedral made earnest and repeated requests to the Duke's heirs to erect a monument, all to no avail, so the money was raised independently. "The renown of his valour had greater power among strangers than had the ties of his blood among kith and kin."

In PW Joyce's *Old Irish Folk Music and Songs,* the ballad of "The Boyne Water" recounts how Schomberg urged William, who had been grazed by a bullet, not to try crossing the Boyne. Undeterred, the king pressed on but it was the Duke who was fatally shot. King Billy, undaunted, urged his men on. "Brave boys," he cried, "be not dismayed/For the loss of one commander;/For God will be our King this day/and I'll be general under." Poor old Schomberg was clearly not a man who commanded great loyalty.

In less acerbic mood, Swift also wrote the memorial to his servant **Alexander McGee**, who died aged only twenty-nine in 1727, "In memory of his discretion, fidelity and diligence in that humble station." It is in the south transept, where an earlier Dean of St Patrick's, **Archbishop Narcissus Marsh** (1638–1713), is also buried. The tablet over his tomb carries an awesome list of his many titles, degrees and appointments.

It was Marsh who, in 1701, founded Dublin's oldest public library. It is beside the cathedral in St Patrick's Close and still going strong. Among the priceless volumes of sixteenth and seventeenth century books is the 1685 translation of the Old Testament into Irish by Bishop Bedell (see Cavan). Marsh received the first fifty copies of Bedell's Bible when it was first published for the use of his students at Trinity College. The first librarian at Marsh's Library, a Huguenot named **Elie Bouhéreau** who had fled La Rochelle in 1685, is buried in the cathedral grounds. One of the conditions for Bouhéreau's appointment was that he donate his private collection of books to the new library. This provoked accusations of simony from Dean Swift who was opposed to the annexation of the role of

Keeper of the Library with ecclesiastic office in the cathedral. However, the Library Bill was passed. Swift lost the argument, Dr Bouhéreau took up his appointment and left his books to Marsh.

Behind the flats opposite the Cathedral Close, there was once a burial ground, now a rather derelict public park, with the odd name of the Cabbage Garden, possibly a corruption of Capuchin. This was the graveyard of the parish of St Nicholas Without (that is to say, without the walls of Dublin) from the late seventeenth century. It was the first Huguenot cemetery in Dublin for the congregation which worshipped at the Lady Chapel in St Patrick's Cathedral. Their badly weathered and broken gravestones now lean forlornly against the walls. One of the founders of the La Touche bank (the fore-runner of the Bank of Ireland), **David Digues des Rompieres de la Touche** was buried here in 1745 and although his gravestone is missing, I was able to decipher several other French surnames of the same period. The inscriptions bear witness to a prosperous city of merchants, clothiers, weavers, hatters and even a sword-cutler all resident in the streets around the cathedral.

The Huguenot graveyard in Merrion Row, just off Stephen's Green, also opened around the end of the seventeenth century and contains many interesting old headstones with French surnames, memorials to the bankers, stockbrokers and merchants of the Huguenot community. The oldest extant and the only one written in French is for a **M Jouglas**, a merchant from Clerac, who died in 1710.

An elaborate stone slab marks the burial place and commemorates **Anne Lunell** who died in 1748.

A follower of the bleeding lamb
Her burthen here laid down
The cross of Jesus pain and shame
exchanging for a stown
True witness for her pardining Lord

Whose blood she felt aplved
She kept the faith, obeyed the word
And lived a saint and died.
Reader her life and death aprove
Believe thy sins forgiven
Be pure in heart, be filled with love
And follow her to heaven.

This sterling lady was the aunt of Olivia Whitmore, the wife of Arthur Guinness, founder of the eponymous brewery.

The Merrion Row cemetery can be visited by arrangement with the Huguenot Trust, 33 Kildare St, Dublin.

CHRISTCHURCH CATHEDRAL

The most famous monument in Christchurch Cathedral is that of **Strongbow**, the leader of the Anglo-Normans who came to Ireland at the invitation of Dermot, King of Leinster, in 1169 and who married Aoife, Dermot's daughter, to seal the Irish-Norman alliance. He died in 1176 when his funeral service was conducted by Laurence O'Toole, the founder of the cathedral and now the patron saint of Dublin.

The original monument over Strongbow's tomb was broken by the fall of the south wall in 1562 and the present one is believed to have been brought by Sir Henry Sidney from Drogheda to replace the original. It probably depicts Thomas fitzJames who was beheaded in Drogheda in 1467. No one really knows the identity of the child-like figure who lies beside "Strongbow" – it may have been part of the original tomb.

From earliest medieval times, Strongbows's tomb was used for the striking of deals, the payment of rents and the exchange of deeds, even apparently for finalising the purchase of a new organ for St Patrick's Cathedral as recently as the end of the nineteenth century. (The names of the surrounding streets, Fishamble Street, Winetavern Street, Skinners Row, tell us that this was the heart of a market area: traders regularly set out their wares in the crypt. In 1678 an ordinance was made against the vaults being used as taverns!)

St Laurence O'Toole (c.1130–1180), the first Archbishop of Dublin, died in Eu in Normandy and was buried there but his heart was returned in 1230 to the cathedral he helped to found. It hangs in an elaborate heart-shaped iron casket in the Chapel of St Laud. Laurence was canonised in 1225. Before coming to Dublin, O'Toole had been the abbot of Glendalough monastery in Wicklow. He was the half-brother of Mor O'Toole, the wife of Dermot MacMurrough, the king who had sought the help of the Normans and whose daughter Aoife married Strongbow.

Down in the crypt, there are several interesting monuments placed there when the cathedral was undergoing restoration in the last century. Among them is a fine marble of the deceased **Nathaniel Sneyd** and his grieving wife. Poor Mr Sneyd *"perished by the hand of violence, the indiscriminating violence of an unhappy maniac."* So the policy of care in the community wasn't working then either.

The mummified remains of a cat and a rat are also on display in the crypt. They met a bizarre death when they got stuck in an organ pipe, the cat in hot pursuit of the rat, and remained there until the organ was being repaired in the 1840s.

St Werburgh's

The dashing **Lord Edward Fitzgerald** (1763–1798), is buried in the crypt of St Werburgh's church. He was a leader of the United Irishmen, the radical group inspired by the recent revolutions in France and the United States. In 1792 he had gone to Paris where he attended the debates of the Convention and was a guest of Tom Paine.

According to Matilda Tone, the wife of Wolfe Tone, writing many years after the rebellion: "It is the truth that Lord Edward Fitzgerald and the Sheares, who had just arrived from France in the heyday of the revolution, were acting revolution before it was made and, joined by all young and ardent spirits, spoke and acted with ruinous indiscretion . . ."

Such indiscretions had serious consequences in a society riddled with spies and informers. Lord Edward Fitzgerald, on the run with the price of £1,000 on his head, was betrayed, captured and mortally wounded in a house in Thomas Street (in the home of a feather merchant) just a few days before the rising was to take place in Dublin. The man who captured and shot Lord Edward, **Major Henry Sirr** (1764–1841), who with Major Sandys and Major Swan ruled the garrison of Dublin, is buried in the churchyard.

Unfortunately, there is no longer any access to the crypt and, from its dilapidated and abandoned air, you may think the church is also closed to the public. However, the keys are available from the caretaker around the corner at eight Castle Street and the church is worth a visit. There is the black Kilkenny marble font where Jonathan Swift was baptised, two early eighteenth century fire engines in the porch and, unusually for Irish churches, interesting old bequests written on the wall.

After the failed rebellion in 1798, the Act of Union was passed so that on 1st January 1801, Ireland became part of the United Kingdom. However, by 1803, England was once more at war with France, and the Irish again attempted to win French help in their struggle for independence. An uprising led by **Robert Emmet** (1778–1803) in July 1803 ended in Emmet's capture and execution by public hanging and beheading at Thomas Street. He is supposed to have been buried in an unmarked site somewhere in Bully's Acre, the public graveyard at Kilmainham. It is perhaps fitting that his grave-site should be in doubt for, in his emotional, impassioned speech from the dock, he said:

"Let no man write my epitaph; for as no man who knows my motives dare not vindicate them, let not prejudice or

ignorance asperse them. Let them rest in obscurity and peace. Let my memory be left in oblivion, my tomb remain uninscribed, until other times and other men can do justice to my character. When my country takes her place among the nations of the earth, then, and not till then, let my epitaph be written."

However, in the course of researching this book, I have come across several accounts of where he might have been buried. In 1887, a headless body was found in a cheap coffin in the Trevor vault in St Paul's Church in North King Street – a Dr Trevor was governor of Kilmainham Jail at the time of his execution. However, the mystery does not end there . . .

St Michan's Church

This churchyard also lays claim to being Emmet's burial place. It is said that he may be buried in the same grave as the United Irishmen, **Rev. William Jackson** (1737–1795), and **Oliver Bond** (1760–1798). It was the raid on Bond's house and the capture of the leaders of the Leinster United Irishmen in March 1798 that had forced Lord Edward Fitzgerald to go on the run. Bond was convicted of treason but died suddenly of a fever while in prison. A curate from St Michan's attended Emmet on the scaffold so there may be some justification in believing that his body could have been brought and clandestinely buried here. (See also Blennerville, County Kerry for another theory.) The other certain occupant of the tomb, Jackson, convicted of high treason, also avoided execution by poisoning himself in the dock.

The crypts at St Michan's are well worth a visit. The church is an old one, built in 1095 on the North side of the Liffey on a marshy site. Because of the very high methane content in the air rising from the remains of an ancient oak forest on which it was built, the air in the crypt acts as a preservative. Down in the vaults, you can see the mummified remains of several bodies, their leathery skin, even their toenails, quite uncorrupted. One of these figures is believed to be a crusader, another a man whose hand has been cleanly cut off.

One vault contains the coffins of the brothers, **John Sheares** (1766–1798) and **Henry Sheares** (1753–1798), executed for their part in the 1798 rebellion, alongside the gruesome and explicit order for their execution by hanging, drawing and quartering at Newgate.

The Sheares brothers were both barristers. They had stayed in Paris for some time during the French Revolution where they had witnessed the execution of Louis XVI. On their return to Dublin they became prominent members of the Society of United Irishmen. Both were considered rather indiscreet and, indeed, they were betrayed by a Captain John Warneford Armstrong of the King's County Militia whom they had recruited into the United Irishmen and to whom they had revealed plans of the rebellion.

Sadly in July 1996, in an act of callous vandalism more reminiscent of an age of barbarian grave-robbers, thieves broke into the vaults of St Michan's, vandalised some of the coffins and their remains and tried to set fire to the church. Firemen managed to douse the fire, the coffins were salvaged from the wreckage and a service of re-interment was held.

ARBOUR HILL CEMETERY

Walking on up along the quays, you will come to Collins Barracks, the new home of the National Museum. Behind the barracks is Arbour Hill Cemetery. This is where the remains of fourteen of the executed 1916 leaders were buried together in a pit of quicklime. After they had surrendered at the end of Easter Week, they were taken to Kilmainham Jail, court-martialled and condemned to death.

The executions were carried out on five days between 3 and 12 May in a bleak high-walled exercise yard where convicts had once broken stones. Each man was led in to the yard at dawn, blindfolded and wearing a white patch over his heart for the twelve men in the firing squad to aim at. Their bodies were then taken to the Arbour Hill Barracks graveyard and covered in quicklime. Here, then, are what remains of the seven signatories of the 1916 Proclamation of the Irish Republic, **Patrick Pearse** (1879–1916), **Thomas Clarke** (1857–1916), **Sean MacDiarmada** (1884–1916), **Thomas MacDonagh** (1878–1916), **Eamonn Ceannt** (1881–1916), **James Connolly** (1868–1916), and finally, **Joseph Plunkett** (1887–1916), who had married his fiancee, Grace Gifford, in Kilmainham Chapel only two hours before his execution. The other men who were executed are buried here too: **Major John MacBride** (1865–1916), Maud Gonne's estranged husband, **Willie Pearse** (1881–1916), Patrick's brother, **Cornelius Colbert** (1888–1916), **Edward Daly** (1891–1916), **Michael Mallin** (1880–1916), **Michael O'Hanrahan** (1877–1916), and **Sean Heuston** (1891–1916).

The site is now a garden of remembrance – the Proclamation of the Republic is carved on the wall behind the pit, in both Irish and English.

Most of the rest of the graveyard has been cleared and the tombstones arranged around the perimeter walls. They mostly commemorate British military personnel, their spouses and children, date from the 1880s and tell their own sad tales.

Arbour Hill is also the site of the Croppies' Acre, the burial place of those executed for their part in the 1798 rebellion. The name "croppy" was given to the United Irishmen because they wore their hair short in the manner of the French revolutionaries – remember this was at a time when powdered wigs were still very much the norm, particularly among the clergy, the legal professions, the universities and in the higher echelons of society.

Among those buried in the Croppies' Acre was **Bartholomew Teeling** (1774–1798), from Lisburn who had joined the United Irishmen in his teens. He had gone to France with Wolfe Tone to help secure French help, served with General Hoche and was aide-de-camp to General Humbert when the French forces landed in Killala in August 1798. Teeling was captured after the surrender at Ballinamuck. He was taken to Dublin, court-martialled and executed at Arbour Hill the following month.

His brother, the journalist Charles Hamilton Teeling (1778–1850) was also a member of the United Irishmen. His valuable account of the revolution was published as a *Personal Narrative of the Rebellion of 1798.*

KILMAINHAM

A memorial plaque on the wall of another exercise yard in Kilmainham names five men who were hanged there on a temporary gallows and whose bones lie "faoi na leaca sa chlós thíos" (under the flags of the yard). They were the infamous Invincibles: Joseph Brady, Daniel Curley, Michael Fagan, Thomas Caffrey and Timothy Kelly, the men who had murdered Lord Frederick Cavendish, Gladstone's new Chief Secretary to Ireland, and his Under-Secretary, Thomas Burke, as they walked near the Vice-Regal Lodge in Phoenix Park on the very day, 6 May 1882, that they had taken up their new positions in Ireland.

A lengthy hunt for the assassins ended with one of the Invincibles informing upon his co-conspirators, reputedly members of a secret militant off-shoot of the Fenians. They were arrested and executed in the following year in May and June 1883.

TRINITY COLLEGE

In a quiet corner, behind the chapel in Trinity College, are buried all the provosts of the college including **Dr Luke Challoner** who was the first provost when the university was founded in the reign of Queen Elizabeth I in 1592 and who died in 1613. A number of people are also buried in the crypts beneath the college chapel including the marvellously eccentric scholar **John (Jackie) Barrett**, (1753–1821). Barrett was College Librarian, professor of Oriental Languages and Vice-Provost. He had a brilliant mind coupled with the most extraordinary ignorance, professing himself astonished at the sight of a sheep ("live mutton!") on a visit to the suburb of Clontarf, the furthest he had been from college since his childhood. He spoke several dead languages fluently but blundered about ungrammatically in English. He was also notoriously mean and filthy, living in dingy rooms on Library Square where he refused to light a fire even in deepest winter and was so ragged in appearance that college staff would mistake him for a vagrant. On his death it was found he had left £80,000 "to feed the hungry and clothe the naked". The trustees of his will decided that his own family, whom he had refused to help during his lifetime, could be deemed to fall into this category and gave them the money.

BALLYBOUGH

Most people passing by a house on Fairview Strand would probably not notice the plaque saying it was built in the year 5616 or know that behind it lies the first Jewish cemetery in Dublin. There had been a small Jewish community in Ireland from the middle ages but apostasy, conversion, emigration and marriage to non-Jews kept their numbers low. In 1690 a number of Sephardi Jews arrived from England to provision King William's troops at the Battle of the Boyne and many of them settled in Dublin afterwards. They included many wealthy merchants, cigar-importers, diamond dealers, teachers of languages, chocolate makers and wholesale jewellers. Until about 1716 the original settlers preferred to be buried in London, where they were considered members of the Bevis Marks synagogue, but a lease for Ballybough was acquired in that year. In 1748 the graveyard was purchased outright by the Portuguese Hebrew congregation of London and presented as a free gift to the Dublin Hebrew community whose numbers were again falling and in some financial distress.

The only extant eighteenth century tombstone is that of **Jacob Wills** (1701–1777), a jeweller on Essex quay, known as "The Frenchman". The tombstone gives the date of his death as 5537 – the Jewish year is calculated by adding 3760 to the Christian year. Many of the early tombstones are believed to have been plundered as the anonymous author of *Excursions Through Ireland* (1816) relates: " . . . (the tombstones at Ballybough) were formerly much more numerous until stolen to be converted into hearthstones and to other purposes; a curious anecdote of this nature is told. A Jew, paying a visit a short time ago to a Christian friend in the vicinity of Ballybough Bridge, found him in the act of repairing his house. Examining the improvements, he perceived near the fireplace a stone with a Hebrew inscription intimating to the astonished Israelite that the body of his father was buried in the chimney."

Ballybough is the burial place of **Lewis Wormser Harris** (1812–1876). Harris would have been the first Jewish mayor of Dublin but he died suddenly on 1 August 1876 just as he was to have assumed office. From Worms (hence the family name Wormser) he had come to Dublin in 1833 where he set up business as a bill-broker and jeweller. He first entered public life as an alderman in 1874, winning his seat with a large majority despite his opponents' attempts to prejudice the electorate against him with anti-semitic slurs. In fact the first Jew to serve as Lord Mayor of Dublin was **Robert Briscoe** (1895–1969) – he served two terms in 1956 and 1961. He is buried in the other Jewish cemetery in Dolphin's Barn.

DRUMCONDRA

Over in Drumcondra on Church Avenue is another lovely little church and graveyard. Here lies the architect, **Sir James Gandon** (1742–1824), responsible for the three finest

Georgian buildings in Dublin – the Custom House, the Four Courts and Kings' Inns. His tomb is of the table-top variety and is situated on the right hand side of the church. He is buried with his friend **Captain Francis Grose**, the antiquarian (1730–1791), who had died unexpectedly in Ireland a month after his arrival here in May 1791 to make a study of Irish antiquities. According to the inscription on the tomb, Grose *"whilst in cheerful conversation with his friends expired in their arms without a sigh."* It goes on to say that he was a friend of Robert Burns and the inspirer of "Tam O'Shanter". Since the poem is about an amorous drunk being pursued by witches, I think we can assume that Grose must have been a colourful and convivial man. Poor Gandon has no epitaph at all, just the one word, *"architect"*.

Patrick Heeney (d.1911), the man who composed the music for the National Anthem, "The Soldier's Song", is also buried in this churchyard. There is a plaque on the wall beside the gate. (See Peadar Kearney, Glasnevin).

There are some very old and unusual stones around the walls, memorials to the Dublin tradesmen of the early 1700s, the weavers, carpenters and brewers "and their posterity" and even one for the Jameson family, the whiskey-makers.

Under the yew tree on the left of the avenue is evidence that gravestones and their inscriptions can provoke fierce passions. A small stone, dated 1900, immediately catches your eye for it is inscribed "Our Lady of the Sacred Heart, Pray For Her. Virgin Most Merciful Intercede", an unusual inscription you feel for a Church of Ireland graveyard. Underneath is written "This stone has been refused admittance to Drumcondra Cemetery On Account of the Above Prayer to the Blessed Virgin, Deceased Being a Roman Catholic." Clearly feelings were running very high when the deceased's family chose to have this inscription added to the stone. For some years the stone was placed outside the church grounds on common land but the appointment of a new rector helped to cool passions and **Mrs McInerney Connor**'s gravestone was allowed to take its place over her grave.

SEAN MCDERMOTT STREET

The **Venerable Matt Talbot** (1856–1925), is the only person "buried" in Our Lady of Lourdes Church in Sean McDermott Street where there is a shrine in his honour. Talbot was an alcoholic labourer who pledged to give up drink and took up religion in a serious way, eating little, sleeping on wooden boards, often attending several Masses every day and giving much of his wages to charity. When he collapsed he was discovered to have been wearing chains under his clothes. He was originally buried in Glasnevin but was exhumed and replaced in Sean Mc Dermott Sreet where his coffin is now on display.

There is another shrine in the Whitechurch, the Carmelite Church on Aungier Street where **Saint Valentine**, a martyr of the early Christian church, lies under the altar. In 1835 Pope Gregory XVI donated the remains of the saint to the Irish Carmelites who brought them to Dublin in a steel casket and re-interred them in their new church. This is the very same Valentine whose feast-day on 14 February is celebrated by the manufacturers of greeting cards, restaurant owners, florists and newspapers proprietors whose papers overheat with pages of tacky lovers' messages. God knows what he did to deserve it.

DEANSGRANGE

Deansgrange Cemetery is in the South Dublin suburbs near Blackrock. Here, in the St Patrick's section, lies that master of the short story, **Frank O'Connor** (1903–1966). A small stone is simply inscribed with his real name, Michael O'Donovan, and his *nom-de-plume*.

In an altogether more ostentatious site, a large quadruple plot with a high marble wall and a bust, is **Count John McCormack** (1884–1945), surely one of the first Irish singers to have enjoyed a hugely successful international career as an operatic tenor and then to have gone on to enjoy equal success as a concert and recording artist. Ernest Newman, a contemporary music critic, once described him as "a patrician artist . . . with a respect for his art that is rarely met with among tenors." The title of Papal Count was awarded to McCormack in recognition of his services to Catholic charities.

Deansgrange also has a small troupe of actors, taking their final rest. They include actor-manager **Anew McMaster** (1864–1962), who forsook an international career to take Shakespeare to the provinces in "fit-ups" from Strabane to Skibbereen – he has a lovely austere headstone designed by Seamus Murphy. The Abbey actor **Arthur Shields** (1896–1970), and his brother Barry, better known as **Barry Fitzgerald** (1888–1961), are buried side-by-side. After a part-time acting career with the Abbey Theatre, Barry Fitzgerald emigrated to Hollywood where he appeared in many films and won an Oscar for his role as Fr Fitzgibbon in *Going My Way*.

Casting a wry eye over them all is Brian O'Nolan (1911–1966), prodigious writer and possessor of many noms-de-plume. As Flann O'Brien, he was the author of *At Swim-Two-Birds*, a novel which appeared in 1939 to a splendid reception from Graham Greene and James Joyce, but the timing was wrong. The premises of the publishers, Longman's, were bombed in the London blitz and stocks of the book were destroyed. Paper shortages prevented a re-print and it was to be many years before his literary star rose again. As Myles na gCopaleen, O'Brien wrote a popular satirical column in *The Irish Times*. He also wrote a column in a provincial newpaper as George Knowall and was known to be fond of writing pseudonymous letters to the newspapers, often making sharp and spirited attacks on the literary establishment.

The grave of **Sean Lemass** (1899–1971), is on the central

avenue on the left hand side. As Taoiseach (1959–1966), Lemass signed the Anglo-Irish Free Trade Ageement with Harold Wilson and instigated the rapprochement with Northern Ireland, becoming the first Taoiseach to meet his Northern Irish counterpart, Captain Terence O'Neill. Earlier, as Minister for Industry and Commerce, he was responsible for the development of many commercial state companies, including Aer Lingus and Irish Shipping.

On the right hand side of the path which leads up from the cemetery office, you will find the monument to the botanist **Augustine Henry** (1857–1930). He was one of those extraordinary Victorians who achieved so much in so many fields. He had first trained as a doctor but went into the Customs Service in China from where he sent back thousands of plants to establish collections at Kew Gardens and the Botanical Gardens in Dublin. He published lists of Chinese botanical specimens with their colloquial names, compiled dictionaries of Chinese dialects, studied law in Formosa and forestry in France. On his return to Ireland he collaborated on a definitive study of the trees of Great Britain and Ireland. He was also active in the Arts and Crafts movement at the beginning of the century and it was he who financed Lily and Lolly Yeats' first business venture.

Others buried in Deansgrange include **John Boyd Dunlop** (1840–1921), veterinary surgeon and the inventor of the rubber tyre filled with compressed air, a development that revolutionised the transport industry.

It is moving to stroll through the oldest section of Deansgrange to read the gravestones of the less famous but no less interesting. Here you will find the memorial of **Richard Waters**, "shot by rebels on his way to the office", on 25 April 1916. At the outset of the 1916 Rising, the leaders had paid scant regard to the protection of civilian life – hundreds of non-combatants died that Easter week. Cemetery records show an application to the registrar for overtime payments to the gravediggers during "the disturbances".

Here too there are dozens and dozens of graves, commemorating the many young men killed in action during the two world wars at Arras, Ypres, Rangoon, Tel-el-Abd and Gallipoli.

DUNDRUM

In his autobiography, William Butler Yeats avoids all mention of his sister Lolly which seems rather callous given that she spent many years of her life working to support the financially strapped Yeats men. **Susan "Lily" Yeats** (1866–1949) and **Elizabeth "Lolly" Yeats** (1868–1940) are buried together in St Nahi's church in Dundrum. Their grave is at the bottom of the sloping graveyard to the left of the church.

In London, Lily the elder sister had worked for the William Morris company, embroidering panels and wall hangings. Lolly had trained as a Froebel teacher, taught painting and published a series of books on "Brushwork". In 1902, the Yeats family had returned to Ireland after countless moves, and with money borrowed from Augustine Henry (see Deansgrange) the two sisters established Dun Emer, "an arts and crafts manufactory", including a printing press which Lolly personally operated. (In the opening chapter of *Ulysses,* Stephen refers to the books "printed by the weird sisters in the year of the big wind.") Later they established Cuala industries which included the Cuala Press. Yeats was the editor but his relationship with Lolly was often explosive. Indeed Lolly's strengths were always being undermined by her brother who believed she had inherited the "mental instability" of the Pollexfens, their mother's family.

All Lolly's life was a struggle to keep the family finances in order and she died still fretting about money and her overdrafts. Ironically, the beautifully produced Cuala books with their lone tree insignia are now prized collectors' items and change hands for huge sums of money.

There is a very fine stained glass window in St Nahi's church by the sisters' friend, the artist, Evie Hone.

DALKEY

The ivy-covered ruins of St Begnet's Church are right in the middle of the main street of the pretty village of Dalkey on the outskirts of Dublin. Its churchyard contains several interesting headstones including a memorial stone to the soldiers who perished when the *Prince of Wales* and the *Rochdale* were shipwrecked on the night of November 18th 1807. The stone is under a tree behind the church but is quite difficult to decipher because of heavy incrustations of lichen.

Both ships had left port in Dublin carrying troops to fight in the Napoleonic wars. The weather was atrocious, with strong gale force winds. A raging blizzard forced the ships to seek shelter but eventually the *Prince of Wales* ran aground on the rocks at Blackrock, having been dragged up and down the coast despite its attempts to anchor. Every one of the 120 recruits was lost as the ship broke up; the captain and his crew escaped on the only lifeboat. He was later to be tried for murder but the case collapsed for lack of evidence.

The *Rochdale*'s fate was equally tragic. It came to grief at Seapoint barely twenty feet from the shore but the weather was so awful and visibility so poor that not one of the 265 men on board could be saved. For days afterwards, bodies from the two wrecks were strewn along the bay. The outcome of these tragedies was that the need for an asylum port in Dublin bay was at last recognised and work began on the construction of the east pier of Dun Laoghaire harbour in 1817.

Look out too for the grave of the self-styled King of Dalkey, **Hugh Dempsey**, who died in 1790. The original Dalkey Festival was set up by a band of eccentric and disorderly students, an early sort of rag week, when they mocked the government and politics of the day and chose a king whose title was "His facetious majesty, the King of Dalkey, Emperor of the Muglins and Elector of Lambay . . . Sovereign of the Illustrious Order of the Lobster and the Periwinkle."

St Begnet's is not usually open to the public but access may be granted on application to the Town Hall next door.

MONKSTOWN

Commander Briggs of the shipwrecked *Rochdale*, (see above) is buried in the old Carrickbrennan graveyard in Monkstown.

Here too are victims of another shipwreck in 1861 when six of the crew of the coastguard vessel, the *Ajax*, perished. Two brigantines had been thrown onto the rocks outside Dun Laoghaire's east pier in a blizzard. Captain John McNeil Boyd and his coastguards were attempting to reach them when a huge wave swept them into the sea.

Their memorial notes that they died *"not on board their ship defending their country but as Christian men seeking to save their perishing brethren. They glorified God whose waves went over them by a death not unmeet for sailors of Christian Britain."* The gravestone is an unusual one, showing a shattered ship's mast and tackle above a square plinth with sculptured panels. There is also a monument on the east pier in Dun Laoghaire where the incident occurred and a statue of Captain Boyd in St Patrick's Cathedral where he was buried in the churchyard with full civic honours.

Carrickbrennan is the final resting-place of **Joseph Holt** (1762–1826), a key figure in the United Irishmen Rebellion. A Protestant who farmed in Wicklow, he had taken the oath of allegiance and had gone on to command 1,200 men at the battle of Ballyellis, near Carnew, where they routed the government forces. Holt evaded capture for many months after the failure of the rebellion, but, with a price of his head, knew he was in mortal danger, not only from the militia who were hunting for him but, as he wrote in his memoirs, from "the spy, the informer and the blood-money man".

In the end, Holt surrendered in November 1798 and was sentenced to transportation to Australia. Like many transportees, he did well there eventually, becoming a bailiff and land-owner. For some reason he returned to Ireland where he lived in Kingstown, a decision he came to bitterly regret. He opened a pub where at first his fame as "the general" attracted much custom but he found it very uncongenial. "One set would call me a bloody croppy and another gang of ruffians would come in and call me a bloody Orangeman," he wrote. He gave up his inn and died a poor man. His monument, which is against the wall on the left hand side facing the playing grounds of the nearby school, was erected by his son Joshua who, it would appear from the inscription, stayed on in Sydney.

This graveyard, by the way, is supposed to be haunted by a Widow Gambol who had betrayed a local priest for reward and was lynched. At present Carrickbrennan is usually locked up: contact the Environment Department of Dun Laoghaire Rathdown County Council if you wish to visit.

As a further reminder of the huge number of victims in the above-mentioned shipwrecks, there is another memorial to those who were buried in Booterstown graveyard. This is a small tranquil walled graveyard hidden behind the petrol station next to the Doyle Tara Hotel on Rock Road. There is open access.

There is a Quaker burial ground on Temple Hill, Blackrock, which much surely be one of the most serene graveyards in the country, with all the rows of identical gravestones standing in the shelter of tall mature trees in a handsome garden. In keeping with Quaker tradition, only the names and dates of the deceased are allowed, with no mention of past achievements or distinguished careers, since all Friends stand equal in the sight of God. One man who lies here is **Alfred John Webb** (1834–1908), the biographer and publisher who wrote one of the first dictionaries of Irish biography, *A Compendium of Irish Biography* (1878).

KILGOBBIN

A hideous cross, like a tree trunk garlanded with roses, wreaths and a bow, stands over the grave of **Richard "Boss" Croker** (1841–1922) in Kilgobbin cemetery, near Stepaside village. The name of Croker is forever linked to the corrupt world of Tammany Hall politics in New York. Croker had emigrated from Cork to the United States with his family when he was three years old during the Great Famine. (Their first home, long since demolished, was on what is now Central Park.) The Tammany Hall Society had been established at the end of the eighteenth century to assist Irish immigrants but soon acquired a dubious reputation for jobbery and corruption. "Boss" Croker entered politics first as an alderman but went on to lead Tammany for seventeen years during which period he acquired a large fortune, ostensibly from a liquor saloon that he owned. He returned to Ireland in 1907, rebuilt Glencairn (now the residence of the British ambassador) and set up racing stables. His horse "Orby", winner of the Derby in that year at odds of 10–1, is buried in the grounds of the house.

SUTTON

On the opposite side of the bay, near Howth, the poet and writer, **Padraic Colum** (1881–1972), is buried in St Fintan's, Carrickbrack Road, Sutton with his wife **Mary Colum** (1884–1957), also a writer. Their epitaph reads:

> *Dream of me there in stirless air*
> *Beyond the seagull's range*
> *Above enshadowed beings we name*
> *Time and loss and change*

Colum was a poet, playwright and novelist. He was born in

Longford workhouse where his father was master: this was the setting of his first novel *Thomas Muskerry* (1910).

It is said that Countess Markievicz's interest in nationalist politics came about when she rented a summer house at Balally in the Dublin mountains and came across Sinn Féin literature left there by Colum, the previous tenant.

In 1914, he and his wife Mary, also a writer, emigrated to America where they taught comparative literature at Columbia University, New York. In 1959 they published a memoir, *Our Friend, James Joyce*. (Joyce referred to Colum as "Padraic what-do-you-Colum".)

The artist **Mainie Jellet** (1897–1944) is also buried here in St Fintan's. Jellet was a friend and colleague of the stained-glass artist Evie Hone (1894–1955) with whom she had studied in London and Paris. As a child Jellet had received her first art classes from Lolly Yeats, the sister of Jack and William. With Evie Hone, she founded the Irish Exhibition of Living Art in 1943. Her austere abstract paintings were revolutionary in Ireland at the time. Her grave is in the oldest section of the graveyard (Section F – 50).

The actor, **Micheál MacLíammóir**, (1899–1978) and his partner, the director, **Hilton Edwards** (1903–1982) are buried side by side in the lawn cemetery area of St Fintan's (plot no. 6–8K). Born Alfred Wilmore in London, Micheál Mac Liammóir made his stage debut in 1911 playing the part of a goldfish in a children's theatre production – his co-star was Noel Coward – hence the name of his roman à clef *Enter A Goldfish* (1977). Alfred re-invented himself as Micheál Mac Líammóir and came to Ireland where he founded the Gate Theatre with Edwards, also an English man. Under their flamboyant partnership, the theatre quickly gained an international reputation, with Edwards as director and Mac Líammóir as actor and theatrical designer. They launched the careers of many world famous actors including Orson Welles who played Othello to Mac Liammóir's Iago. Mac

Liammóir's last performance was in December 1975 in *The Importance of Being Oscar,* the one-man show compiled by him and directed by Edwards which had proved immensely popular with audiences all over the world.

The old Abbey Churchyard, in Howth, contains many interesting old tombstones. The key to the abbey itself is available at 13 Church Street. Inside, under a protective canopy, is a richly carved altar tomb with the effigy of the knight **Christopher St Laurence** (d.1470) and his wife. There is also a tombstone in memory of a casualty of the famine, **William Hancock** (d.1848), a magistrate, land agent and Poor Law Commissioner, "who made such unwearied exertions in seasons of famine and pestilence that he fell a victim to the third attack of fever caught in the discharge of his official duties."

Nearby in Howth is the cromlech, a large unhewn stone, which is reputed to mark the grave-site of the princess **Aideen** (d. c.285), who died of grief when her husband Oscar, son of Oisin and grandson of Finn McCool, was slain in battle at Tara. Her grave is on a pathway among the rhododendron groves on the hill behind the Deerpark Hotel. Aideen's Grave was the subject of a poem by Sir Samuel Ferguson in which a sorrowful Oisin laments a future when the ogham of Aideen's name will have worn away from the stone and all the Fianna are forgotten. Until, "a child of chance" – perhaps you or me – walking on the hill of Howth finds the grave

> *And gazing on the cromlech vast*
> *And on the mountains and the sea*
> *Shall catch communion with the past*
> *And mix himself with me.*

KILDARE

It is not only the graves of saints that become shrines or places of pilgrimage. The grave site of the United Irishman, **Theobald Wolfe Tone** (1763–1798), has had the status of a shrine since shortly after his death. He is buried in Bodenstown, against the southern wall of the church, the gravestone now protected behind gates. This is actually the third slab put up over his grave, both the original and its replacement having been chipped away by over-enthusiastic relic hunters. On the wall behind the grave, Patrick Pearse's words on Tone are written:

Thinker and doer, dreamer of the immortal dream and doer of the immortal deed, we owe to this dead man more than we can repay him . . . to his teaching we owe it that there is such a thing as Irish nationalism and to the memory of the deed he nerved his generation to do, to the memory of '98, we owe it that there is any manhood left in Ireland.

Inspired by the republican ideals of the French Revolution, Tone had assembled an expeditionary force of the French Army to invade Ireland and end British rule. The first two attempts having been abandoned in 1796 and 1797 because of severe storms, a small force under General Humbert eventually landed at Killala on 22 August 1798. They were forced to surrender after only two weeks. Meanwhile Tone himself had set sail for Lough Swilly, unaware of Humbert's failure, and this fleet was also attacked and defeated. Tone was taken to Dublin where he was court-martialled and condemned to death, though since he was an officer of the French army and had never held a commission in the British army, his court-martial was illegal. At his trial, which he attended in the dress uniform of a French officer – a large cocked hat with broad gold lace and the tri-coloured cockade, blue coat with large gold epaulets and pantaloons with gold-laced garters – he denied none of the charges, declared that he had never any recourse other than to "open and manly war" and gave evidence of his French army commissions. His request to be shot was turned down. Rather than submit to an illegal hanging, Tone attempted to commit suicide in his prison cell with a smuggled pen-knife. He died a week later.

Matilda Tone (1769–1849), who married Wolfe Tone when she was only sixteen, died in the United States. She was buried in Georgetown, Washington, and later re-interred in the Green-Wood Cemetery in Brooklyn where, in 1996, the President of Ireland, Mary Robinson, unveiled the restored monument over her grave.

MAINHAM

There is a monument outside the Anglo-Norman church at Mainham which still sounds as petulant and bitter as when it was first erected. **Stephen Browne**, the heir of Castle Browne, now Clongowes Wood school, wished to build a family mausoleum inside the church grounds but the rector and Browne fell out. The slab over the mausoleum tells of the acrimony that arose from Browne's intention to erect the monument in the church :

> . . . & S^d Browne applyd sever-
> al times to his parishminister ye Revd John
> Daniel for his consent wch he refused-
> him unles s^d. Browne would give him
> Five guineas for soe doing. A Gentleman

whose character is remarkably well kno-
wn as well as his behaviour on several
occasions to s^d Browne & ye onely
Clergyman in ye diocese whose
passion would prevent their church
to be Imbelished or Enlarged, & to de-
prive themselves and their successors
from ye burial fees; and he has been
ye occasion of oblidging s^d Browne
to erect s^d Monument here on
his own Estate of Enheritance
Wth s^d Browne think proper
to insert here to shew it was
not by choyce he did it.
May ye 1st 1743

The "s^d. Browne" died in 1767 and is buried in the mausoleum with his wife, parents and other members of his family. You can peer in and see the elaborate altar tomb topped with a pair of gruesome skulls as *memento mori*. The mausoleum stands at the outer wall of this very attractive old churchyard but can now be reached through it. There are some very old and interesting graves here, with burials dating back to the early 1700s.

Mainham has long been an important site. It was the site of the aonach, or royal assembly, of the Kings of Leinster and is believed to be the burial place of a **Queen Baun** in AD 31.

BALLITORE

Ballitore is an unusual little village founded as a Quaker settlement in the eighteenth century when a Yorkshireman, **Abraham Shackleton** (1697–1771) opened a school there. Its pupils were to include Edmund Burke, Henry Grattan and Napper Tandy. The author **Mary Leadbetter** (1758–1826), Shackleton's niece and the postmistress of Ballitore for many years, wrote the annals of Ballitore, a fascinating account of eighteenth century life in a Quaker community in Ireland, including descriptions of the civil unrest in 1798.

The Quaker burial ground is signposted and is just outside the village enclosed within a high boundary wall in a field. It is an austere place, with simple stones which bear no inscriptions other than the name and dates of the deceased, but was delightful when I visited it in springtime with daffodils and primroses in profusion. Some of the stones are difficult to read because of the white lichens. Abraham Shackleton, the founder of the school, and Mary Leadbetter are both buried here.

In her annals, Leadbetter writes of the harrowing impact of the rebellion in the summer of 1798. One afternoon, as her husband and herself were having tea at home in Ballitore, an alleged informer, **Richard Yeates**, son of Squire Yeates of Moone, was "brought in a prisoner, his yeomanry coat turned . . . One of his (captors) went to the table and helped himself to bread and butter, looked at himself in the mirror, and remarked it was "war time". The prisoner, with tears trickling down his cheeks, spoke sadly of his seven children; his guards sought to console him by telling him he was "an honest Roman" and should not be hurt . . . (but) presently we heard a shot . . . he was taken into a house, and in spite of his own entreaties, the endeavours of many others to save him, and even the efforts of Priest Cullen who begged the life of the young man on his knees, he was murdered, piked and shot."

Soon afterwards Mary and a friend were shocked to come across the murdered body of Richard Yeates lying behind a wall. In an interesting comment on the aftermath of the rebellion, she remarks that "for several months there was no sale for bacon cured in Ireland, from the well founded dread of the hogs having fed upon the flesh of men."

In 1945, in a pit near Moone Abbey not very far from Ballitore, workmen discovered the skeleton of a man and a rusty pike head. The body is believed to be that of the murdered Richard Yeates.

There is now a small museum in the Old Meeting-house of Ballitore which tells the history of the Quaker village, including copies of letters written by young boarders at the school.

The polar explorer, **Sir Ernest Shackleton** (1874–1922), a descendant of Abraham Shackleton, was born near here in Kilkea House. He died suddenly on his fourth Arctic expedition and was buried at South Georgia Island.

(Another gruesome 1798 story is told about the Drummer's Well outside Narraghmore, just east of the Pike Bridge where a major battle took place in 1798 between the Kildare pikemen and the Suffolk Fencibles. A few hundred yards up from the bridge, a plaque marks the spot of **The Drummer's Well**, where a drummer boy who had been drafted into the English army was killed. He was brought up in England, the son of a republican-minded Irish mother who taught her boy how to beat out secret signals on his drum. Drafted into the Fencibles at the age of twelve and sent to Ireland, his allegiance was clearly in doubt for at the battle of the Pike Bridge he beat out a cryptic message to the Irish to let them know the English forces were running out of ammunition. Unfortunately, an officer of the Suffolks recognised the signals, had the drummer boy shot and threw his body into the watery grave of the well.)

CASTLEDERMOT

There is a unique Viking gravestone in the churchyard at the Church of Ireland in Castledermot. As you go through the remains of the Romanesque archway, you will find it over on your right. It resembles a solid granite coffin but is actually a representation of a typical Viking long house. It is decorated with a cross and other carvings and there is nothing quite like it anywhere else in Ireland.

Here too is a grave of the ninth century Munster king and

Bishop of Cashel, **Cormac MacCullenan**. Castledermot is a treasure-house of the stone-mason's art. As well as the remarkable Viking gravestone and the archway, there are two tenth century high crosses with terrific carvings, a round tower and a holed "swearing stone", a curious mixture of pagan fertility stone and Christian cross.

There is another oddity in a side chapel in the ruins of the Castledermot Franciscan Friary – a macabre cadaver tombstone dating from the sixteenth century. It carries a representation of the aptly named **James Tallon** and **Joan Skelton** – their shrouds are pulled back to show the skeletons beneath with worms coiling around the ribs. A lizard-like creature has the male skeleton's foot in its mouth. The key to the friary is available from the house next door.

Nearby, in the rath of Moone, there is a damaged limestone slab which commemorates **Thomas Ashe** who, for reasons now lost in the mist of time "was interred here at his own request nine feet deep the 30 June 1741".

OUGHTERARD, NEAR NAAS

Sir Arthur Guinness (1725–1803), the founder of Guinness's brewery at St James's Gate in Dublin, is buried in a vault inside the ancient ruins of the Church of St Brigid in Oughterard with his wife Olivia and other members of the family. The epitaph reads:

> *They lived universally beloved and respected*
> *And their memory will long be cherished*
> *By a numerous circle*
> *Of friends, relations and descendants.*

There can be little doubt of that. His descendants surely have great reason to cherish both his memory and his foresight in taking out a 9,000 year lease at St James's Gate in Dublin. No one at the time could have foreseen that the name Guinness would become so inextricably linked with that of Ireland, a classless drink which seems to be part of the national culture, equally at home at hurling matches, race courses, oyster festivals and even in maternity wards.

NAAS

Until recently there was a striking red stone tomb-slab set in the aisle of St David's Church at Naas marking the grave of **Joshua Carpenter** (1585–1655), the steward of the notorious Wentworth, Lord Deputy of Ireland, the arrogant and provocative governor of Ireland between 1633 and 1641 during the reign of Charles I. When Wentworth was arraigned on a charge of treason and executed, members of his staff, including Carpenter, were flung into prison. Almost forgotten by his friends at court while the Civil War in England raged, it was not until four years later that the charges against Carpenter were finally withdrawn. He was released to live out the rest of his life at Jigginstown though the curious inscription on the tomb says he died in "Elsinowre" in Denmark on 2 March 1655.

Sadly, during recent renovations to the church, the gravestone had to be lifted from the aisle and was broken. At present, it is sitting in large pieces behind the altar on the right hand side. It is to be hoped such an unusual and ancient stone will be restored and replaced where the public may read it.

Somewhere in St David's churchyard is the unmarked grave of **William Nevison**, or Swift Nix, an infamous English highwayman who had fled to Ireland to escape arrest, lived in the now ruined seventeenth century house at Bishopscourt, and died in 1688.

JOHNSTOWN

On the outskirts of Naas, in the churchyard of the pretty village of Johnstown, lies the body of **Richard Southwell Bourke** (1822–1872), sixth earl of Mayo, but better known as The Pickled Earl. Bourke had served as Chief Secretary for Ireland before being appointed Viceroy and Governor General of India in 1868. While carrying out an inspection of a penal establishment there, he was assassinated by a sepoy.

His untimely death presented his staff with a problem. He had requested that he should be buried in Johnstown – how could they return a body on a lengthy sea journey in hot weather? The solution they came up with was to immerse the earl's body in a barrel of rum and so he duly returned to Ireland. After his funeral which was attended by the great and the good, toasts were raised to "the Pickled Earl" and the epithet has stuck. One shudders to think what they drank to toast him. The grave is in a large railed enclosure with a Celtic high cross.

KILCULLEN

Sir Dan Donnelly (1786–1820), the bare-knuckle fighter, beat the reigning English champion at what is now called Donnelly's Hollow at the Curragh of Kildare in a lengthy and bloody fight. He made and squandered a fortune from his fights but died young. He was buried at Bully's Acre in Dublin but his body was snatched by medical students. It was later purchased by a Dublin surgeon who removed the arm – "the longest arm in the history of pugilism" – to study its musculature. The rest of the body was safely re-interred but the arm had a less restful history, being first kept in a Scottish medical school, then bought by a travelling circus owner for exhibition, then purchased by Texas McAlevey, an Ulster bookie. It has now ended up in a glass case in The Hideout Inn in Kilcullen along with other memorabilia of his life. The pub is awash with other dead and unburied creatures – tigers, leopards, bears, deer and even a pair of swans.

RATHANGAN

In the Protestant church in Rathangan, don't miss the gravestone of **Thady Doorly** who, according to the inscription, died aged 140, his death "hastened by an accident"! Clearly someone could not resist vandalising the stone by added the extra "1".

KILKENNY

St Canice's Cathedral contains some of the finest Elizabethan tombs in the country, many of them the memorials of the influential Norman family, the Butlers, whose principal seat was Kilkenny. They were descendants of the Norman knight, **Theobald Fitzwalter**, who was given the hereditary title of *Le Botiller* in 1185. This made him a sort of royal toastmaster, but, more importantly, gave him the right of *prisage*, a tax or butlerage on all wine cargoes landed in Ireland.

The Butler monuments in black Kilkenny marble are outstanding. In the south transept, a large double tomb of Piers Butler shows him dressed as a knight lying beside the figure of his wife Margaret who is wearing a most extraordinary twin-peaked head-dress. He was the first Earl of Ormonde to be buried in the cathedral. Another tomb is that of their son Richard who died in 1571; yet another is the effigy of Alicia Butler, a vowess, or holy woman, who lived in the first half of the sixteenth century. The frontispieces of these altar-tombs are superbly decorated with sculptures of cheerful smiling bishops and saints.

Another impressive marble tomb of the same period is that of **Nicholas Walsh**, Bishop of Ossory, (d.1585). Bishop Walsh pioneered the use of Irish typefaces in printing and made the first translation of the New Testament into the Irish language. Unfortunately, he met an unhappy and untimely end, murdered in his palace for proceeding in a case against an adulterer.

Life in the seventeenth century could be unpredictable and dangerous for many reasons. On the wall opposite, there is a monument to a mother, **Mary Stoughton**, who died in child-birth in 1631, and to her baby son Henry.

A vertuous mother and her new-borne Sonne
parted ere tomb and end where they begun
Shee from her bearing-bed, hee from the wombe
Exchanged their living graves for this dead tombe
This pile and Epitaph seeme vainly spent
Goodness reares her a surer monument
No curious hand can cut, no lab'ring head
Bring more to praise her than the life shee lead
Bemone that readest! and live well (as shee)
Soe shalt thou want nor tombe nor elogie.

The Kyteler slab is the oldest grave slab in the cathedral. It was found during recent restoration work under a pavement. Translated from Norman French, it reads:

Here lies Jose de Keteller
Say thou who passeth here a prayer
who died the year of grace
One thousand two hundred and four twenties.

This is confidently thought to be the father of the notorious **Dame Alice Kyteler**, the fourteenth century Kilkenny witch. She was prosecuted for sorcery, accused of holding "nightly conference with a spirit called Robert Artisson" and for sacrificing to him "in the highe waie nine red cocks and nine peacocks' eies." She married four times and is thought to have murdered her husbands. (Her second husband, **Adam le Bund,** is buried in the grounds of the old church at Callan.) Although several of her accomplices came to a very unpleasant end – one of her maidservants was publicly burned at the stake – Dame Alice managed to evade capture and was smuggled out of the country to England. Her house, the oldest building in Kilkenny, is now Kyteler's Inn.

There are many more ancient and unusual grave-slabs set in the aisles of the cathedral where they were re-laid during restoration of the cathedral after its destruction by Cromwell. They show the tools of the trades of the deceased: the Carpenter, the Cobbler and the Weaver. There is also a gravestone showing a representation of the Cock in the Pot similar to that in Lismore Cathedral in Waterford.

BURNCHURCH

Opposite the well preserved fourteenth century Norman tower in Burnchurch, in the grounds of the Church of Ireland, lies the body of **Henry Flood** (1732–1791), orator and statesman, and illegitimate son of Warden Flood, the chief justice of the King's Bench.

Henry Flood became Member of Parliament for Kilkenny and the borough of Callan in the Irish House of Commons and was for many years Leader of the Opposition. He was regarded as the most outstanding orator of the day, a passionate advocate of constitutional reform and resistance to British control over Irish affairs. However, he didn't always settle his arguments with persuasive rhetoric. As often as not he threw down a challenge to a duel. On one occasion he killed his electoral opponent, James Agar, and was brought to trial for murder. He was acquitted. Later he lost the leadership of the opposition to **Henry Grattan** (1746–1820), an episode marked by a dramatic row on the floor of the House which would have ended in a duel but for the fact that both Flood and Grattan were placed under arrest. Flood's grave is a horizontal slab with a raised crucifix at the rear of the church. Henry Grattan is buried in Westminster Abbey.

CALLAN

On the outskirts of the town of Callan, signposted about

one mile south on the Clonmel road, are the communal graves of all those who died in Callan workhouse during the Great Famine. The graveyard is in a field enclosed by a dry-stone wall. There are no headstones but a plaque at the entrance gate was erected in 1986 by the Callan Heritage Society in memory of "the uncounted victims of famine and poverty buried here, most of whom died in Callan workhouse, 1841–1922." Within the graveyard itself, there is another stone monument erected in 1994 as part of the Great Famine Project in memory not only of the Irish victims but to all those who have died in famines in Bangladesh, East Timor, Brazil, Ethiopia, Somalia and Angola. "Their memory challenges us to work for a more just and equitable world." The engraving shows a man crucified on a cross made of a spade and fork.

KILREE

A high cross at Kilree reputedly marks the grave of **Niall Caille**, a high-king of Ireland who was drowned in the river at Callan in 844, though this may well be romantic conjecture because of other local associations with the king. According to popular legend, the river was in full spate, the king's servant got carried away and Niall himself perished as he tried to rescue him. The river is now called Abhainn Ri "The King's River" and Kilree, at first glance, may look as if it means The King's Church but none of this can be satisfactorily authenticated. However, the tall sandstone cross is of the right period. It is decorated with representations of stag-hunting and a chariot, of Daniel killing the lion and Daniel in the Lion's Den. It stands in a field behind the ruins of the monastery and the round tower.

JERPOINT

Many will be surprised to learn that **St Nicholas** is buried in Ireland but here he is lying in the ruined church of an abandoned medieval town just west of Jerpoint Abbey. It appears that Norman crusaders from Jerpoint retreating from the Holy Land exhumed the remains of St Nicholas at Myra and finally returned to Ireland with them after a stop-over in France. The grave is marked by an unusual slab, quite unlike anything I have seen elsewhere. It is a large reddish-brown stone, lying on the ground, with a relief carving of a monk in habit and cowl. Unfortunately it was broken in two when a fir tree fell upon it a few years ago.

This site is accessible only with permission from the present owner, Joe Teesdale, on whose property the church stands. The church, at present being cleared of the ivy which has engulfed it, is one hundred years older than Jerpoint Abbey. The area here by the river was once the site of Newtown-Jerpoint, a medieval town no trace of which remains, but the bumpy terrain is suggestive of the covered over traces of the houses, mills and brewery that were once here.

Nearby in Jerpoint Abbey, one of the finest monastic ruins in Ireland, there are many wonderful sculptured tombs, including that of the first abbot, **Bishop Felix O'Dullany**, who died in 1202. The effigy is holding a crozier gnawed by a serpent, one that St Patrick obviously missed. There is an admission charge.

KILFANE

Opposite the Church of Ireland church there is a gate to a path that leads up to the ruins of an earlier church founded by St Paan. Mounted on the wall inside is a striking sculpture of a Norman knight in full chain-mail. His legs are crossed, he looks over his shoulder and carries in one hand a shield which bears the Cantwell arms. The effigy is known as the Cantwell Fada – the long or tall Cantwell. Originally this sculpture may have been the cover of a tomb, possibly of **Thomas de Cantwell**, the founder of this church, who was described in contemporary annals as being very old in 1319. The sculpture is extremely well-preserved despite its great age, having been buried underground for many years.

On the wall opposite the Cantwell Fada is a well-preserved ancient gravestone commemorating a **Richard Lee** who "died of small pox in 1707, aged forty-two, leaveing only one son of three years old." His epitaph tells us:

> *Rarely is justice done ento the Just*
> *In his case of necessity it must*
> *C'Ause you'll speake well or silent be*
> *He was composed of love and charity*
> *A bright example to posterity*
> *Reader if in his paths you'll rightly tread*
> *Doubt not of being hapy when your Dead.*

GRAIGUENAMANAGH

Duiske Abbey in Graiguenamanagh is one of the earliest Cistercian foundations in Ireland. On the wall to the right of the door inside the church is an effigy of the Norman **Knight of Duiske**. It is not as well preserved as the Cantwell Fada but he is still an impressive sight in his full regalia and chain-mail. This stone carving probably lay over his grave.

There are also two ancient high crosses in the churchyard and many old stones of interest. One is a memorial to the **Tierney family** who all died of cholera in July 1826 with its poignant inscription:

"in youthful bloom we were doomed by God's command
to leave this gloomy, poor, unhappy land".

TINNAHINCH

A strange inscription is erected on the tomb of **John Patsull** at the old church of St Michael's, Tinnahinch, near Graiguenamanagh. It reads as if the sculptor was not paying full attention to the task in hand and has omitted a line or two.

> *Great King of Glory, Justice, Mercy, Peace,*
> *I vilest sinner of the Human Race*

Thou has prevented, my Request thou hast given
it is of thy mercy infinite that I am among the liven.
Glory be to the father and to the Son, and to the Holy Ghost.
John Patsull. Aged 78. 1776.

No longer "among the liven", John Patsull's identity is something of an enigma. There was a Patsull from Graigue who worked as a land surveyor and several old maps made by him still survive. Map-making was an important skill for landowners who needed to have accurate measurements in order to charge rents to their many tenants and sub-tenants. However, local tradition also suggests that Patsull, or possibly the map-maker's son, may have been an apostate priest, a Catholic who became a parson before re-adopting Catholicism. Perhaps because of this, the tomb became an object of fear. In the early nineteenth century when the end of the tomb was partly broken and open to the elements, one man reported that he saw Patsull's eyes watching him from the empty sockets of his skull as he passed through the churchyard.

INISTIOGE

Inistioge is often cited as the prettiest village in Ireland. In the graveyard of the church beside the tree-lined square is the mausoleum of the poet **Mary Tighe** (1772–1810), the author of *Psyche* and the beautiful wife of the owner of the Woodstock House demesne, Henry Tighe MP. The neo-classical sculpture inside the mausoleum is an effigy of Mary asleep under the protective gaze of Psyche, the allegorical lover of Cupid. The mausoleum is on the left behind the church and may be viewed on application for the key from the church warden.

Poetry in Inistioge was not confined to Mary Tighe – there are many amusing poetic inscriptions on the headstones both in the churchyard and mounted on the wall beside the door.

LAOIS

ROSENALLIS, NEAR MOUNTMELLICK

After the battle of the Boyne in July 1690, the defeated Irish dispersed around the countryside with the English soldiers in pursuit. These irregular soldiers and pikemen, known as rapparees, plundered the towns and villages they passed through in search of food, shelter and, doubtless, revenge. One of the houses that they besieged and burned was the home of **William Edmundson** (1627–1712) at Rosenallis, near Mountmellick.

William Edmundson was originally from Westmoreland in England. He had fought under Cromwell in Scotland and at the battle of Worcester and came to Ireland around 1654 in search of new opportunities. A recent and charismatic convert to Quakerism, he was the first person to set up a regular Friends' Meeting, first in Lurgan, then settling with other families at Rosenallis on the edge of Slieve Bloom. He was a most courageous and admirable man, suffering persecution and imprisonment for his radical beliefs. He toured Ireland, Britain, America and the West Indies preaching the Quaker cause.

The rapparees who surrounded his house in 1690 captured him and his two sons and were about to kill them. Edmundson challenged them to show how he had wronged any of their countrymen, protesting that, on the contrary, he had done his best to save them. He refused a blindfold, declaring that he would look them in the face as they shot him as he was not afraid to die. Finally, a local chief called Dunne intervened and they were reprieved. Mrs Edmundson was not so lucky. She was stripped and turned out on the road and died later as a result of exposure. Edmundson and the other Quaker families moved into Mountmellick until 1691 when he was able to return to his farm at Rosenallis. He remarried at the age of seventy-one.

He is buried in the Friends' burial ground, the oldest Quaker graveyard in the country located on the outskirts of Mountmellick at Rosenallis on land that he had donated. A plaque on the wall tells us "Near this spot is buried William Edmundson, the first member of the Society of Friends who settled in Ireland. Died 31st of 6th Month 1712 (old style) aged nearly 85 years."

The Society of Friends went on to become a reforming force in Ireland. Resolutely pacifist, they opposed the compulsory payment of tithes to the established church and founded many excellent schools. During the famine years they took a leading and exemplary role in the provision of relief.

LONGFORD

EDGEWORTHSTOWN

The novelist **Maria Edgeworth** (1767–1849) is buried in the Edgeworth vault in the grounds of St John's Church of Ireland in the parish of Mostrim, or Edgeworthstown as it is now known, where her father owned a large estate. Her first novel, *Castle Rackrent* (1800),with its extravagant cast of hard drinkers, skinflints, heiresses, gamblers and a woman locked in a dilapidated castle for seven years, was an outstanding success. She was much admired by Walter Scott who wrote in the preface to the first edition of *Waverley* that he was attempting "to emulate the admirable Irish portraits drawn by Maria Edgeworth". Both he and Wordsworth came to Edgeworthstown to visit her.

Her father, **Richard Lovell Edgeworth** (1744–1817), is also buried in the family vault. He was a remarkable man, a member of Grattan's parliament, a prolific writer, botanist, pioneer of women's education and the inventor of a semaphore which could communicate messages from Dublin to Galway in eight minutes. He married four times and fathered twenty-two children. With all these dependents, it is hardly surprising to discover on reading his daughter's memoirs that he was careful with money.

She writes that he had come to Ireland in 1782 "with a firm determination to dedicate the remainder of my life to the improvement of my estate and to the education of my children; and farther with the sincere hope of contributing to the melioration of the inhabitants of the country from which I drew my subsistence." He found Edgeworthstown House in a lamentable condition. "Doomed to a place where nothing sublime or beautiful could be found he used to comfort himself by considering that it was the better for his family . . . if he had been placed in a charming situation he might have felt irresistible temptations to expensive improvements."

In his will he left instructions for his burial: "I would have neither velvet, nor plate, nor gilding employed in making my coffin, which I would have carried to the grave without a hearse by my own labourers." He wanted no monument nor inscription other than a marble tablet similar to the one he erected for his own father inside the church and carrying nothing but the year of his birth and death.

There are memorabilia of the Edgeworths on display in the church and a table which was presented to Maria by Walter Scott on his visit to her.

The graveyard of St John's is full of interesting stones. Look for the grave of a woman called Burnett who died at the age of 116 in 1787 (round the back of the church) and for the unusual memorial to **Arthur Henry**, a boy of fourteen accidentally shot at a circus in 1892. The memorial is a truncated stump of a pillar standing on a plinth, signifying that Arthur too was cut down. A sister of Oscar Wilde is also buried here.

The graveyard contains many famine graves marked only with a small rock – this area was severely affected by the famine. In 1846, Maria Edgeworth informed the Society of Friends who were gathering information on the state of the country and on the need for relief programmes, that of the 5,000 inhabitants in the town, 3,000 were in need of relief and that fever and sickness were common. Maria Edgeworth herself took a prominent role in caring for the starving and the sick and in setting up the relief programmes.

LOUTH

MELLIFONT

Mellifont Abbey was the first Cistercian abbey in Ireland, founded in 1142 by a community of French monks sent from Clairvaux – they returned home very soon afterwards, as St Bernard explained, because of the ill discipline of the Irish. Eventually a rather reluctant second contingent was prevailed upon to return and presumably put manners on the Irish monks!

It was to Mellifont that **Dervorgilla**, (d.1193), a wealthy benefactress of the abbey, retired after a turbulent life and died in the nuns' convent. She was the wife of Tiernan O'Rourke, the chieftain of Breifne, but had been abducted in 1152 by the king of Leinster, Dermot MacMurrough. Abduction is rather a strong word in the circumstances as it appears she was not unwilling to leave her husband in retaliation for his cruelty towards her and she remained with Dermot for a year. In any case Dermot compounded the insult to O'Rourke when he put up no resistance to her recapture. In the years that followed, as Dermot's strong alliances broke down, O'Rourke pursued him, marched on his castle at Ferns and burnt it down. This precipitated Dermot's plea to the Anglo-Norman King Henry to come to his aid in Ireland in his bid to secure the High Kingship. The rest, as they say, is history.

Dervorgilla retired to a life of prayer in the nunnery where she is buried though there is no marked grave. She was responsible not only for endowing Mellifont but for financing the building of the wonderful Nuns' Church at Clonmacnoise in County Offaly.

DUNLEER

For a man so eminent and so controversial, it is surprising that **John Foster** (1740–1828), the last Speaker of the Irish House of Commons, also lies in an unmarked grave.

Foster opposed the Act of Union in 1800 which disbanded the Irish Parliament and made Ireland part of the United Kingdom. At the last meeting of the House, he refused to give up the mace, the symbol of his authority. This was kept in the family until 1937 when it was acquired at auction by the Bank of Ireland in College Green in Dublin (the Bank now occupies the old House of Commons).

Foster was also a fierce opponent of the 1793 Catholic Relief Act and of Catholic Emancipation. As an inducement to surrender the influential post of Speaker, he had twice been offered a peerage but, despite the fact that his wife accepted the title of Baroness in 1790, Foster himself held out until 1821 when, on the coronation of George IV, he finally accepted the title of Lord Oriel and Baron of Ferrard. He died at his seat in Collon and was buried in the Church of Ireland in Dunleer. One must assume family disagreements led to his grave remaining unmarked.

DROGHEDA

Saint Oliver Plunkett (1625–1681) is not actually buried in St Peter's Church, Drogheda, although his severed head is on display in an elaborate casket. He was Archbishop of Armagh at a time of violent persecution of Catholics and was forced into hiding for six years in 1673. Falsely accused of trying to foment rebellion by Titus Oates – in the so-called Popish plot – he was arrested and imprisoned first in Dublin and then in Newgate Prison in London where, after a travesty of a trial, he was executed on 11 July 1681. He was canonised in 1975. Other relics of Plunkett are enshrined at Downside Abbey in England.

MAYNE

Old archaeological journals and county magazines are a mine of information about old gravestones and memorials recorded by enthusiastic antiquarians in the early years of this century. Many may well have disappeared by now. I cannot confirm that the affectionate inscription over the grave of one **Paddy Ward** in the churchyard at Mayne, six miles from Drogheda, is still in existence. It is quoted in the Louth Archaeological Society Journal for 1938.

> *Beneath this stone here lieth one*
> *That still his friends did please*
> *To Heaven I hope he is surely gone*
> *To enjoy Eternal ease*
> *He drank he sung while here on earth*
> *Lived happy as a Lord*
> *And now he hath resigned his breath*
> *God rest him Paddy Ward*
> *He departed this life Sep. the 12th 1793*
> *Aged 65 years. Here also lieth the Body of Owen Ward*
> *who depd this life 1781 aged 26 years . . . by the author.*

It reminds me of an equally convivial gentleman, Thomas Davies who died in 1760, and who is remembered on an English tombstone in Stanton Lacy in Shropshire:

> *Good natur'd, generous, bold and free*
> *He always was in company*
> *He loved his bottle and his friend*
> *Which brought on soon his latter end.*

MEATH

NEWGRANGE

Newgrange must surely be the gravesite that attracts most visitors in Ireland. Built about 5,000 years ago, it is the most impressive of the three great prehistoric burial mounds in the Boyne Valley in an area known as Brugh na Bóinne or the "Palace of the Boyne". This location could be said to be the cradle of Irish civilization with evidence of the neolithic society who first occupied and cultivated this valley scattered all around. It remained the spiritual and political centre of Ireland until the arrival of Christianity when the nearby Hill of Tara, the seat of the High Kings, began to lose its pre-eminence.

The single tomb at Newgrange is a passage about twenty metres in length leading to a conical-roofed chamber and two side-chambers, the entire structure covered over with a cairn of stones and tons of earth. Large kerbstones surround the exterior wall, many of them beautifully decorated, particularly the stone at the entrance.

It was not until the excavations during the 1960s that archaeologists discovered that the whole tomb is aligned with the rising sun on the morning of the winter solstice when light penetrates through the unique roof-box at the entrance and illuminates the burial chamber. The farmers who built this tomb about 3,000 BC without benefit of metal tools clearly had highly developed artistic, engineering and architectural skills and a strong cohesive community. Why then does a visit to Newgrange today often disappoint? Is it that restoration of the white quartz retaining wall, though perfectly authentic and using materials scattered around the site when it was excavated, somehow makes the whole place look like some sort of phoney interpretative centre rather than the real thing? Or perhaps it is simply that the whole place is usually crowded with visitors and endless queues for admission. See it, if you can, in mid-winter when the solemnity and mystery of the place becomes more apparent and you can summon up the sense of the men and women who once were interred here.

Who was buried here remains a mystery. It was popularly believed to be the burial grounds of the gods of the Tuatha de Danann, the mythical race who came to Ireland from overseas, and later of the Kings of Tara, and while each of these traditions are improbable, it is equally certain that these extraordinary structures could not have been erected to house the remains of the ordinary toilers and labourers of the Boyne valley of 5000 years ago but must once have been the sacred grounds where the chieftains or priests were laid to rest.

Dowth and Knowth, the other passage-graves mounds in Brugh na Bóinne, may also be visited but not entered. In both, there are two passage-graves. Finds from these sites may be seen in the National Museum.

LARCH HILL

For originality or eccentricity in his choice of tomb, you have to hand it to **Mr Watson** of Larch Hill. A wealthy landowner and enthusiastic huntsman, he began to fear that he might have killed one fox too many and that he might therefore be condemned to return to earth as a fox, in which case it would be wise to prepare a covert.

He instructed his staff to build a huge dome-shaped burial chamber, or "earth", on the lawns outside his house. It was covered over with turf and topped with a pepper-pot tower, and it was there, after his death some time in the mid 1800s, that he was interred. For added security, the local hunt was barred from the area and his widow continued to leave out food for him beside his grave. Larch Hill is a private house but is open to the public at certain times of the year when other Watson follies – a small-scale Stonehenge, a miniature castle and a tower built of cockle shells – can be seen.

OFFALY

CLONONY

Under a tree in the grounds of the now ruined castle of Clonony, four miles east of Banagher, one mile west of Cloghan, is a slab commemorating **Mary** and **Elizabeth Bullyn**. They were second cousins of Queen Elizabeth, the daughter of Anne Boleyn, the executed wife of King Henry VIII. The huge limestone slab which is over eight feet long and a foot thick was discovered in 1803 by workmen excavating stones when building the nearby canal. It reads:

here under leys Elisabeth and Mary Bullyn daughters of Thomas Bullyn son of George Bullyn the son of George Bullyn Viscount Rochford son of Sr Thomas Bullyn Erle of Ormond and Willsheere

After Henry's execution of his wife, he had the whole Boleyn (or Bullyn) family "attainted", or outlawed and many of them fled to Ireland. Little is known about Elizabeth or Mary or their exact date of death but matching portraits owned by Birr Castle of two beautiful young ladies in Elizabethan dress are thought to be of them.

BIRR

Birr Castle was the home of the astronomer **William Parsons**, third earl of Rosse, (1800–1867), the builder of the Leviathan, then the largest telescope in the world, for the observation of the planets. He was internationally renowned particularly for his study of nebulae and was decorated by Queen Victoria, Napoleon III and the Imperial Academy of St Petersburg.

His wife, **Mary, Countess of Rosse**, was no less innovative, being an early pioneer of photography. Her dark room in the castle is the oldest extant in the world. The Earl and Countess are buried in the family mausoleum in the old St Brendan's Church on William Street, Birr. At present this very overgrown graveyard is not open to the public but the key may be made available on request from the Castle Estate Office.

The Leviathan telescope has recently been restored and is exhibited in the castle demesne as part of the Birr Science project to celebrate the achievements of the Earls of Rosse in the fields of astronomy, engineering and botany. Lady Rosse's dark room, complete with her collection of chemicals and photographs, is also to be put on display.

EGLISH

The writer **William Bulfin** (1864–1910) is buried in Eglish churchyard, a few miles outside Birr. Bulfin emigrated to the Argentine in 1884 where he worked on the estate of another Irish emigrant and wrote for *The Southern Cross*, a weekly Buenos Aires newpaper for the Irish community there. He published an account of his experiences in *Tales of the Pampas*. He returned to Ireland after a seventeen year exile and undertook a journey around Ireland by bike which he wrote about in the still very readable *Rambles in Eirinn*. A handsome charismatic man, known as Che Bueno, he had an immense love of Ireland and an infinite stock of stories: in the preface to *Rambles in Eirinn*, he is described by his editor as "a social as well as a national tonic". In the plot of the grave one is surprised to see a memorial wreath "in loving memory of William Bulfin from Buenos Aires Hurling Club", apparently still going strong to this day!

A plaque alongside is dedicated to **Eamonn Bulfin**, (d.1968) who is also buried here. He was the commander of Patrick Pearse's Rathfarnham company during the 1916 Rising and, according to the inscription, "was privileged to raise the Irish flag over the GPO on Easter Monday morning 1916."

The area around Eglish suffered badly during the Great Famine and many of its victims are buried in this graveyard. A memorial points out that the population of the townland was 6,644 in 1841. By 1851 it had fallen to 4,841.

BANAGHER

In a plot enclosed by railings in St Paul's churchyard (N.E. corner) lies **Reverend Arthur Bell Nicholls** (1818–1906), the husband of Charlotte Brontë, with the inscription:

> *Until the day breaks and the shadows flee away*
> *In Loving Memory of Rev. Arthur Bell Nicholls,*
> *Formerly Curate at Haworth, Yorkshire.*

Charlotte had finally accepted a proposal of marriage from Arthur in 1854 despite opposition from her father, Patrick Brontë, to whom she said, "Father, I am not a young girl, not a young woman even – I never was pretty. I now am ugly. At your death I shall have £300 besides the little I have earned myself . . . " Around the same time, she also wrote to Mrs Gaskell: "My destiny will not be brilliant . . . but Mr Nicholls is conscientious, affectionate, pure in heart . . . I am very grateful to him." The newly-weds travelled to Banagher for their honeymoon at Cuba Court where Arthur's uncle was headmaster of a Royal Free School.

Contrary to all expectations, the marriage was a happy one if short-lived. Charlotte died the following year from complications during pregnancy. Before her death she revoked her will which would have left all her estate to her father and now bequeathed everything she had to her husband "the tenderest nurse, the kindest support – the best earthly comfort that ever woman had." Arthur stayed on at Haworth until Patrick's death six years later when he returned to Banagher. In 1864 he married his cousin, Mary Anna Bell, and lived to the ripe old age of eighty-eight.

CLONMACNOISE

Clonmacnoise is one of the most important early monastic

sites in Ireland. It stands in a magnificent location on the banks of the river Shannon. It was founded by **Saint Ciaran** in 598, right at the crossroads of Ireland where the main esker route running east to west across the country meets the river Shannon, the main north-south route. A year later he died of plague and was buried in what is now known as St Ciaran's oratory, a shrine and place of pilgrimage since his death to the present day.

Clonmacnoise flourished for many hundreds of years, surviving raids by the Munstermen, the Vikings and the Normans until it was finally demolished by the English garrison at Athlone in 1552. The annals tell us "Not a bell large or small, an image or an altar, or a book or a gem or even glass in a window left was not carried away." Fortunately over 700 grave slabs were left, many of which can still be read. Most date from the period 800–1000.

The tradition of laying a stone over a grave became established centuries earlier in Ireland than in the rest of Europe. The earliest examples were primarily intended as grave markers as they are not full body size. It is difficult to authenticate the exact identity of the monks and craftsmen whose lives were commemorated by these stones, but, most of them would have commemorated the more distinguished abbots, craftsmen, scholars and kings. Many of them are inscribed with a request for a prayer like the one which reads "Or do Odran hua Eolais" – pray for Odran who had knowledge; Odran was a scribe whose death was recorded in the Annals of Clonmacnoise in 994.

Many kings were buried here. The O'Conor kings of Connacht had burial rights in the monastic city and had their own mortuary chapel built about the year 1000. The last High King of Ireland, **Rory O'Conor** (d.1198), was granted the honour of burial within the cathedral itself at the north-east corner of the chancel. The elaborately sculptured High Cross of the Scriptures is now indoors but once marked the grave of **King Flann**, the High King of Ireland who died in 915.

There is an entrance charge to the site.

KINNITY

On an elevated site to the right of the Church of Ireland is the unusual pyramid-shaped Bernard family vault. The Bernard family had originally come to Ireland during the Cromwellian wars and established themselves first in Carlow. In the mid-1700s they moved to Kinnity where they restored the castle and laid out the town.

Captain Richard Wellesley Bernard had served in the army in Egypt and, inspired by the pyramids there, started building his own pyramid in 1830. It is quite a sight to behold in the middle of the Irish midlands. A doorway leads down a flight of steps to a passage underground where six bodies have been interred, including Captain Bernard himself.

In the porch of the church there is an unusual carved ninth century slab, richly decorated with spirals, similar in style to some of those at Clonmacnoise. This is thought to have been the tomb slab of an abbot of Kinnity, possibly a poet/historian called **Colpan MacConaghan** whose death was recorded in the annals in 871. There had been an abbey on the site since 557. The key to the church is available from Peavoy's shop at the corner.

There is an even more important cross nearby in the grounds of Kinnity Castle Hotel, formerly the home of the Bernards. This cross was dedicated to **King Maelsechnaill**, the King of Tara best remembered for capturing and drowning Turgesius, the leader of the Vikings in Ireland who had sacked Armagh and advanced up the Shannon with a large fleet plundering all the churches in the Shannon basin. The cross would once have stood in the old Kinnity Abbey.

TULLAMORE

The tiny Kilcruttin cemetery in the park opposite the courthouse in Tullamore was the burial place of thousands of paupers and famine victims who had sought refuge at the Tullamore workhouse during the 1840s. The local clergyman reported in 1852 to the Board of Guardians that it was so full that "no more bodies can be interred there without greatly endangering the healthfulness of the neighbourhood. In one corner more than one thousand paupers have been buried within the last few years and two hundred have been laid there in the last year."

In 1806, the King's German Legion were stationed here, members of a corps of exiled Hanoverians who became mercenaries in the British army after the fall of Hanover to Napoleon. There are two memorials to these men, one to Rifleman **Christophe Koch** who died in a riot in the town on 26 July 1806 and another, a tall pillar, to **Frederick William Baron Oldershausen** (1776–1809) of the German Dragoons. This latter one has recently been restored by a Tullamore-based German company. The German inscription is translated as follows:

The bonds of husband, father, friend
Are early loosed in a foreign country
Thou sleepest the solemn sleep of death
This monument speaks no lie.
The graving-tool of truth carves these lines
Thou wert true, noble, loyal, brave.

CLONBULLOGUE

Jasper Robert Joly (1819–1892) bequeathed his entire collection of manuscripts and printed volumes to the Royal Dublin Society with instructions that they should be handed over to the National Library of Ireland as soon as one was established. The collection of over 20,000 volumes, unbound papers and prints, is one of the jewels of the Library and includes such invaluable material as the *Journals of Captain Cook* (1772), books on Irish topography and history as well as Napoleonic literature.

A precocious child, Joly had entered Trinity College as a scholar at the age of thirteen and graduated when he was just eighteen. Although called to the Bar, he never practised and dedicated his life to books. He is buried in the Joly plot in Clonbullogue Church of Ireland churchyard.

WESTMEATH

One of the most eccentric graves in Ireland is that of **Adolphus Cooke**, who died in 1876 at the age of eighty-four. He is buried in a beehive-shaped tomb, twelve feet high and forty-two feet in circumference, set in a moat in an abandoned churchyard in Bracklyn. (The church and its cemetery are situated on the grounds of the Beehive Lodge, a pub and night club now closed. To reach the graveyard, you go through the main gate and follow the small path leading off to the right. The church has been bricked up and the tall trees, bramble and rampant ivy give the place a suitably Gothic atmosphere.)

Eccentric as it is, the beehive-shaped tomb was not Cooke's first choice of burial place. He had had a marble book-lined vault built where he wanted to be placed after his death, embalmed and seated at a writing-desk in front of a fire which was to be kept continuously alight. However, the local rector of Killucan would have none of this and Cooke was buried in the beehive folly he had erected as a mausoleum for his father and where Mrs Kelly, his nurse, is also interred.

Adolphus Cooke was the natural son of his father and inherited the property only when his two half-brothers predeceased him. He promptly began to run his estate in a most unconventional style. He believed in reincarnation and, convinced that his late father had returned to earth as a turkey, instructed his men-servants always to raise their hats and the maid-servants to curtsey when the turkey strutted into view. He would frequently challenge his bull to a fight and ordered his men to build nests for his crows.

Cooke had made several wills, the last of which left his estate to a younger son of the Earl of Longford (from the nearby Pakenham estate) but the will was contested by a former beneficiary on the grounds that Cooke was of unsound mind. The trial and appeal dragged on for years so that by the time Pakenham won the case (with the judge of the opinion that a belief in reincarnation did not necessarily make a man mad) the estate was bankrupt.

TRISTERNAGH

Lovers of abandoned churches, old stones, arches, ivy and moss will also like to visit the very old tomb of the Elizabethan settler, **Sir Henry Piers** (d.1620) who is buried in a ruined roofless church at the entrance gate of Tristernagh Abbey, a few kilometres outside Ballynacarrigy. Henry Piers was among those sent to colonise Ireland by Queen Elizabeth after the Battle of Kinsale. He was the Governor of Carrickfergus Castle for a time but was later granted lands in Westmeath.

TYRELLSPASS

James Daly (1900–1920) is buried at Tyrellspass. He was the leader of the Indian Mutiny in 1920 when Irish soldiers serving with the British Army mutinied in protest against the Black and Tan atrocities in Ireland. Daly was among those executed – his remains were returned to Ireland by the National Graves Association in 1970. The tombstone inscription is written in Irish:

I ndíl cuimhne
Shéamus Uí Dálaigh
a rugadh 1900
Treoraí na Ceannairce Indiacha

a chuireadh chun báis
faoi ordú na Sasanach I bpriosún
Dagshai ar an tarna la de mhí
na Samhna 1920
Go dtuga Dia suaimhneas síorai da anam.

During the War of Independence, a guerrilla war was waged against the British Crown forces, characterised by attacks on police barracks and ambushes by "flying columns" of volunteers. This met with savage reprisals, particularly by the ex-soldiers recruited as Royal Irish Constabulary auxiliaries, the so-called "Black and Tans", who set fire to towns and businesses, looted and engaged in revenge beatings and shootings.

There is a monument to all the men who died or were executed in the Indian Mutiny in the Republican plot in Glasnevin Cemetery in Dublin.

WEXFORD

FERNS

The small village of Ferns was once the capital of Leinster and the home of the Kings of Leinster. In the ruins of the cathedral behind the new cathedral is an ancient stone, the decorated shaft of a larger cross, which is believed to be the grave marker of **King Dermot MacMurrough** (1110–1171), the man who changed the course of Irish history. Described by Giraldus Cambrensis in his jaundiced description of Ireland as "nobilium oppressor, humilium erector", Dermot in fact ruled his territory from 1126 until his death wisely and well, keeping it relatively stable during a period of protracted unrest and inter-provincial wars in Connaught, Munster and Meath. He skilfully combined political ambition and strategic alliances with support for the church, granting it lands to establish new monasteries and priories which he then endowed.

Of course he could be ruthless too – his first known exploit was the rape of the abbess of Kildare in 1132, he had seventeen kinsfolk blinded in 1141 and he famously abducted Dervorgilla, the wife of his enemy Tiernan O'Rourke (see Mellifont, County Louth). When thwarted in his bid for the High Kingship he had the audacity to invite Henry II to send a Norman force to Ireland, sealing the alliance by marrying his daughter Aoife to the Norman leader, Strongbow. In unprecedented disregard for Irish custom, he then granted the whole of Leinster to Strongbow as Aoife's dowry. Dermot clearly intended to make himself High King with the help of his Norman allies in return for accepting the overlordship of Henry; however, his unexpected death in 1171 changed everything and allowed the Normans to seize sovereignty. Another hostile chronicler in *The Annals of Ulster* recorded his death thus:

Dermot, King of the Province of Leinster, after destroying many churches and territories, died in Ferns without Extreme Unction, without Communion, without Penance, and without a Will, in reparation to Columcille and Finian and all those saints besides whose churches he destroyed.

A plaque on the wall of the new cathedral tells us that the first bishop of Ferns and the founder of the first church here, **Saint Edan** (also known as St Moague) died in 632 AD at an advanced age and is buried under the cathedral floor.

KILLANN

Memorial statues of Father John Murphy of Boolavogue, of pikemen and croppy boys and the defeated heroes of the battle of Vinegar Hill, stand in the centre of many Wexford towns, towns which witnessed so much blood-letting and hundreds of public executions during the United Irishmen's rebellion of 1798. Over 30,000 people are estimated to have lost their lives in the county of Wexford alone so the graveyards of the county are filled with the graves of the insurgents and the yeomen.

The youthful **Captain John Kelly** (1776–1798), commemorated in the song "The Boy from Killann" is buried in Killann churchyard opposite St Anne's Church. His monument, erected in 1898 by the '98 centenary committee, is a tall Celtic cross within a railed enclosure. The inscription says that he was wounded while leading the insurgent troops at the battle of New Ross, taken prisoner and "most cruelly executed at or near the old bridge".

The battle of New Ross, one of the bloodiest of the summer of 1798, took place on 5 June when the town was successfully defended against the rebels led by Kelly and Bagenal Harvey, effectively preventing the spread of the rebellion into the province of Munster.

In the graveyard of the Church of Ireland on the other side of the road is the grave of **Moira O'Neill**, (b.1870) the pseudonym of **Agnes Nesta Shakespeare Higginson**, the poetess of the Glens of Antrim.

New Ross

After the defeat at Vinegar Hill, **Beauchamp Bagenal Harvey** (1762–1798), the wealthy lawyer and landowner of Bargy Castle who had been Commander-in-Chief of the rebel army, managed to escape capture but was subsequently arrested hiding out in a cave on the Saltee Islands with Dr John Colclough. Both men were taken to Wexford, court-martialled and executed. He was buried in Mayglass cemetery in Killinick, near New Ross. The inscription on the plaque on the wall of the old church declares "Is aoibhinn agus is coir bas d'faghail ar son an duteais" – the Irish translation of *dignum et decorum est pro patria mori*.

The head of **John Henry Colclough** of Ballyteigue Castle, spiked on Wexford courthouse railings after his execution, was rescued and secretly buried in the churchyard of the now ruined old church in St Patrick's churchyard in Wexford city (key available at Municipal Buildings) where there are many other graves of men who died in the rebellion.

Many more United Irishmen are buried in St Mary's churchyard in New Ross, a graveyard that has been thoroughly mapped and researched by local historians, and which contains the graves of many victims of plagues, famines and rebellion. In the ruins of the ancient church there are also several wall and floor tombstones of the thirteenth century, including that of **Isabella de Clare**, (d.1220), the daughter of Strongbow and the wife of William le Mareschal who founded the church in 1207. The key is available at No. 6 Mary Street.

BALLYFAD

Another key figure and victim of the 1798 rebellion is buried in Ballyfad, near Gorey. A liberal Protestant of independent fortune, **General Anthony Perry** (d.1798) had joined the insurrection with other Wexford gentlemen like Dr John Colclough and Bagenal Harvey. He commanded an army of 34,000 men who marched against the government troops at Arklow in June. In Teeling's *Personal Narrative of the Rebellion*, he is described as running an extraordinary military campaign "which would not have dishonoured a more experienced veteran in arms." However, he was arrested and treated brutally, his hair cropped, rubbed with gunpowder and set alight. He was released from this ordeal and subsequently sought to restrain the cruelty and mayhem of his own troops as they broke up in disarray. Perry was re-arrested and hanged at Edenderry on 12 July 1798.

BUNCLODY

In 1875 workmen working on widening the bridge across the Slaney discovered a mass grave containing many skeletons. These were thought to be the bodies of the men who fell in the battle of Newtownbarry in 1798. They were re-interred in St Mary's Cemetery. The inscription reads: "God Save Ireland. Erected to the memory of the Patriots of '98. 1875." A plaque is also situated near the bridge where the bodies were found.

WEXFORD

John Redmond, (1856–1918), Parnellite and Leader of the Irish Party at Westminster who secured the successful passing of the Home Rule Bill in 1912, is buried in St John's graveyard, John Street, in the family vault. Redmond was completely taken aback by the ferocity of Carson's opposition to Home Rule and by the formation of the Ulster Volunteers who were prepared to fight tooth and nail to maintain the Union between Great Britain and Ireland. With the formation of the Irish National Volunteers, things might well have drifted towards civil war but for the outbreak of the First World War which effectively put all question of Home Rule on the back burner. Redmond was equally dismayed by the Rising in Easter 1916 and the proclamation of a republic. He favoured Home Rule within the British Empire.

KILMYSHALL

About half a mile outside Kilmyshall, near Bunclody, there is a little graveyard (reached by walking through a field of turnips!) which is the final resting place of a great beauty from Clonmullen Castle who inspired the love-song "Eibhlín, a rún" or "Eileen Aroon" (My darling Eileen). The grave of **Elenor Booth** is at the bottom of the sloping cemetery and is marked with an old weathered slab which reads "Hear lieth the body of Elenor Booth also Kavanagh who died the 14 day of June 1717 aged 63."

The love-song was written by the poet Cearbhall Ó Dálaigh. He had been married to a very beautiful woman but overheard two men say that Elenor was even more beautiful. The poet promptly abandoned his wife and pursued Elenor. Accounts differ as to whether they lived happily together or, according to one version, if he was murdered by the family of his first wife.

It is a beautiful poem, clearly irresistible to "Eileen."

Le grá dhuit níl radharc im chionn,
a Eibhlín, a rún!
Bheith ag trácht ort is saibhreas liom,
a Eighlín, a rún!
Mo mhóráil róghrinn is tú,

> *sólás na soillse is tú,*
> *mo ghreann is mo mheidhir is tú,*
> *a Eibhlín, a rún*

(With love for you, I have no sight in my head, Eileen Aroon. Riches for me is talking about you, Eileen Aroon! My real glory you are, the solace of light you are, my fun and my merriment, you are, Eileen Aroon!)

An Eileen Aroon music festival is held in Kilmyshall every year.

TINTERN ABBEY

To have lived in an age when a challenge to a duel was considered an honourable reaction to a real or imagined slur was hazardous enough without the additional handicap of being shortsighted. In 1807 a duel took place between **John Colclough** and William Alcock. They were friends, both gentlemen of fortunes, both electoral candidates for the county and both very near-sighted. Only William Alcock had spectacles.

Despite the presence of twelve magistrates, the duel was allowed to go ahead without any attempt to halt the proceedings. Colclough was killed instantly, as both General Thomas Cloney and Sir Jonah Barrington testified in their eye-witness accounts. He was buried in the dramatic ruins of Tintern Abbey following a huge funeral, attended by no less than 15,000 horsemen, footmen and a procession of carriages. For the eighteen miles from Wexford to Tintern Abbey, "no man could be heard to raise his voice higher than his breathing" according to Cloney.

WICKLOW

Robert Halpin (1839–1894), was master of the ship that laid the transatlantic cable from Valentia Island to Newfoundland. Born in Wicklow, he had gone to sea at the age of ten and rapidly moved up the ranks. In 1865, he was appointed master of the *Great Eastern,* the iron ship designed by Isambard Kingdom Brunel and then the largest ship in the world. He set out from Valentia Island, off the coast of Kerry, to lay the cable but, over 1,600 miles out to sea, the cable broke and the project had to be abandoned. Halpin returned one year later, repaired the cable and completed the task. Subsequently he laid the cables between France and Newfoundland, Bombay and Suez, Madras and Singapore, Australia and Indonesia, a total of 23,000 miles.

After such an eventful life he retired to his home in Wicklow, Tinakilly House, where he died of gangrene poisoning after cutting his toe. He is buried in the Church of Ireland parish church in Wicklow in the Halpin family plot where his epitaph reads

They that go down to the sea in ships
That do business in great waters
These see the works of the Lord.

There is also a granite obelisk memorial in Fitzwilliam Square in Wicklow which describes his many achievements.

DERRYLOSSARY
Erskine Hamilton Childers (1905–1974), the fourth

president of Ireland, is buried in a small country churchyard near Roundwood. His grave is marked with a simple granite cross and a recumbent slab with the prayer:

> *God be in my head and in my understanding*
> *God be in mine eyes and in my looking*
> *God be in my mouth and in my speaking*
> *God be in my heart and in my thinking*
> *God be at mine end and at my departing*

President Childers had served thirty-five years as a Fianna Fáil TD, holding ministerial rank on several occasions and serving as Tánaiste (deputy prime minister) until 1973 when he was elected to the presidency. The following year he died suddenly. Childers was the son of Erskine Childers, executed in 1922 during the Civil War.

GLENDALOUGH

Saint Kevin (d.618) came as an anchorite to the remote and inhospitable valley of the two lakes, Glendalough, some time in the sixth century. As his reputation and accounts of his visions spread, other hermits joined him until Glendalough became one of the most important monasteries of the time. It continued to flourish as a school of learning and site of pilgrimage, although often sacked by Vikings, Normans, and not least, by local marauders. It was finally burnt out in 1398.

The Reefert Church was one of the most sacred places in the whole monastic settlement. Its name Rígfert, "the Cemetery of the Kings", comes from the fact that the local Leinster kings of the Uí Máil and and the Dál Messin Corb were buried here. Saint Kevin, who was himself of royal blood, was almost certainly buried in the graveyard next to the church when he died at a great age in 618.

A pattern, or popular religious festival, used to be held in Glendalough on the feast-day of Saint Kevin despite the church's attempts to stamp it out. Patterns were rowdy affairs, a day of dancing and drinking and general merry-making. Entertainers of every variety turned up and hawkers would set up their stalls among the antiquities and the gravestones. There were games, tug-of-war competitions, boxing, and then inevitably as the day progressed, fights, disorderly conduct and, doubtless, "immoral behaviour". The tradition of the pattern eventually faded away, its demise hastened by the crusade of the Temperance Movement in the 1830s and the famine years that followed.

BLESSINGTON

On the morning of 18 April 1941 during the Second World War a Handley Chase Hampden plane crashed at Blackhill near Ballyknockan, killing outright all four of the young Royal Air Force crew: the wireless operator, the air gunner and two pilots. They are buried side by side in a corner of St Mary's Church of Ireland churchyard on the main street in Blessington. The four identical stones bear their names, number and rank, the RAF insignia and their ages – the youngest was only nineteen, the oldest twenty-three.

GLENCREE

It was not only British airmen who crashed and died in Ireland. During both world wars, many German airmen, civilian detainees, merchant seamen and sailors were killed on Irish soil or in Irish waters. In 1959, the German War Graves Commission opened a cemetery in Glencree and all the dead, who had been scattered all over the country and even on off-shore islands, were re-buried together in this place.

It is a lovely setting in an old quarry with the fast-flowing Glencree river running alongside. In among the beds of heather are stone crosses and granite slabs bearing the names of the dead in pairs. Here are some of the victims of the *Arandora Star* which sank off Tory Island on the early morning of 2 July 1940 when it was torpedoed in broad daylight by a German U-boat. The ship was carrying civilian internees from Great Britain to Canada. There were over 1,000 casualties, most of them Italians, though many Germans too. Here too are the graves of German airmen who veered off-course and crash-landed in Ireland; there is the grave of a young man who parachuted into Wicklow by accident, was arrested locally but before he could be handed over to the authorities took cyanide and killed himself. At the rear of the cemetery, on the right, is the grave of the spy, **Dr Hermann Gortz**, who also committed suicide when captured by the Special Branch in 1947. There is a memorial Hall of Honour to all the dead with the following inscription:

Take your sons for ever to your heart, sorrowing mothers –
Know and believe the fact that love overcomes all boundaries.
Further the craving and plea of the Dead who rest in this place:
See, that over the world the Star of Peace may arise!

ENNISKERRY

The artist, **Paul Henry** (1876–1958), is buried in St Patrick's Church on the outskirts of Enniskerry in a wooded churchyard dominated by tall fir trees. The grave is marked by a low headstone of rough-hewn granite. Henry, who had studied in Paris and in Whistler's studio, is best remembered now for his landscapes and portraits of the people of the West of Ireland, particularly those of Achill Island where he lived for seven years. He lost his sight in 1945. His autobiography *An Irish Portrait* was published in 1951.

The pioneer aviator, **Captain Patrick Saul** (1894–1968), is also buried here. His first action-packed career was as a sea captain. He sailed several times around Cape Horn and commanded a gun boat on the Tigris during the First World War. In the late 1920s he turned to flying and in 1930 was the navigator on the historic east-west trans-Atlantic flight from Dublin to Newfoundland. He held a commission in the Royal Air Force during the Second World War but returned to Ireland as chief of air traffic at the flying-boat station at Foynes, County Limerick and later at Dublin.

DELGANY

A massive white marble monument in the Church of Ireland in Delgany commemorates the many members of the

La Touche family who are buried in the vault here, including Peter La Touche of Bellevue who died in 1828 aged 95 and who had financed the building of the church in 1789. Peter La Touche was the grandson of David de la Touche, a Huguenot who had come to Ireland with William of Orange and stayed on, founding the first bank in Ireland and establishing a prosperous weaving industry in the Liberties area of Dublin.

The family was pre-eminent in the country's commercial and political life for over two hundred years. At the time of the 1798 Rebellion, there were no fewer than five La Touche members of the Irish Parliament. (Four of them, including Peter, voted against the Act of Union.)

It was to Peter La Touche that the 1798 rebel, Joseph Holt, (see Carrickbrennan, Dublin) surrendered after his period on the run. His wife, Mrs Elizabeth La Touche, paid for the hire of a coach for Mrs Hester Holt and her children to Cobh and for their passage to Australia when Holt had been sentenced to transportation. One of the Holts' children, Marianne, then aged seven, remained behind and was educated at the orphanage for young girls that Mrs La Touche ran in the grounds of the house at Bellevue. (The house was demolished in the early 1950s and Delgany golf club now occupies the estate grounds.)

KILMOLIN

And finally for something completely different before leaving Wicklow. On the road between Glencree and Enniskerry, you may be startled to see a sign-board for the Kilmolin Pet Cemetery. It is exactly that, Ireland's only graveyard for the family pet, set upon a hill overlooking the Wicklow Mountains. There are hundreds of small perfectly tended graves with headstones or plaques recalling the virtues of Buster, Patch, Lady, Ketchup and Chutney and a menagerie of other dogs, cats, rabbits and apparently even a pigeon. Almost the first one you will see, under a tree near the entrance gate, proudly proclaims: "Fluffy, the best mouser in Bray", as heartfelt a memorial as any other in this book.

MUNSTER

CLARE

Brian Merriman (c.1749–1805) is buried in an unmarked grave in the cemetery about half a mile outside Feakle though there is a bronze commemorative plaque. Merriman, a hedge schoolmaster and small farmer, was the author of the epic, *The Midnight Court,* a long bawdy poem in Irish about a trial in which the shortcomings of contemporary men, both in bed and out of it, are frankly debated by a formidable tribunal of women. They are angry that "the youth of the country's gone to hell", that young men won't marry and women in their prime "drop unplucked from the boughs of life" or are forced into marriage with old men "without hope in body or help in limb". In the end, the judge declares:

> *I do enact according then*
> *That all the present unmarried men*
> *Shall be arrested by the guard,*
> *Detained inside the chapel yard*
> *and stripped and tied beside the gate*
> *Until you decide upon their fate.*
> *Those that you find whom the years have thwarted*
> *With masculine parts that were never exerted*
> *To the palpable loss of some woman's employment,*
> *The thrill of the milk and their own enjoyment;*
> *Who having the chance of wife and home*
> *Went wild and took to the hills to roam,*

Are only a burden on the earth
So give it to them for all you're worth.
Roast or pickle them, some reflection
Will frame a suitable correction.

(translation by Frank O'Connor)

The poem has been translated by many writers including Frank O'Connor, Thomas Kinsella, David Marcus and Lord Longford and has been adapted for the stage. Its explicit celebration of sex led to its being banned in its English version even at a time when it was freely available in government publications in Irish. An annual summer school in celebration of the poet has been held in Feakle every August since 1968. It is popularly known as "The Lark in the Clare Air".

MILTOWN MALBAY

Recent years have seen an explosion of all manner of summer schools which attract people to celebrate the life and work of any number of literary figures, discuss urgent political and philosophical matters and generally indulge in a bit of "craic". One of the most popular is held in Miltown Malbay in honour of the traditional Irish musician and folklorist **Willie Clancy** (1918–1973). Clancy's music was hugely popular, not only in Ireland, but throughout Europe and the USA. He led the renaissance of interest in traditional music and instruments such as the uilleann pipes, the bodhrán and the tin whistle. His grave, by the right hand wall in the local cemetery, is marked with a handsome granite slab with an inset relief of the seated musician playing the pipes. His name is given as Liam Mac Fhlannchadha.

KILLIMER, NEAR KILRUSH

Ellen Hanly, the victim of a notorious murder in 1819, is buried in Killimer graveyard. Her melodramatic life and death inspired Gerald Griffin's novel, *The Collegians,* which in turn became the basis for Dion Boucicault's play, *The Colleen Bawn*, and Benedict's opera, *The Lily of Killarney*. A Reverend W Fitzgerald "who knew her in life and saw her in death" also wrote about her in *Ellen Hanly: The True History of The Colleen Bawn* (1868). In more modern times, Brian O'Nolan adopted the persona of Myles na gCopaleen, the outlandish storyteller in *The Collegians*, as the protagonist of his long-running column in the *Irish Times*.

Ellen Hanly was a young girl of sixteen who was persuaded to steal some money from her uncle and elope with an absolute cad called John Scanlon. They went through a mock marriage (his servant disguised as a priest conducted the ceremony) but soon afterwards Ellen Hanly disappeared. The personalities and a trail of coincidences seem tailor-made for an opera, from the intervention of the Knight of Glin in a dispute over the possession of a cloak pawned for a bottle of whiskey, the discovery of a shallow grave in the sand near Money Point, through to the closing act with the defiant "husband" going unrepentant to the gallows and his accomplice's statement that he had earlier been ordered to drown Ellen on a trip to visit antiquities on an island on the Shannon estuary. John Scanlon was defended in court by Daniel O'Connell but was found guilty of murder and hanged at Limerick. His manservant was arrested some months later and hanged for the same offence.

(Gerald Griffin abandoned his writing career in his thirties, destroyed his manuscripts and joined the Christian Brothers in Cork where he died of typhus two years later in 1840.)

There is a regular car and passenger ferry between Killimer and Tarbert.

POULNABRONE

No visit to County Clare would be complete without going to see the Poulnabrone Dolmen, a striking portal tomb dating back more than 4,000 years which stands proudly in the heart of the extraordinary landscape of the Burren. Its graceful sloping capstone stands on two immense pillars. All around it between the crevices of the limestone pavement is a startling diversity of tiny flowers.

CORCOMROE ABBEY, NEAR BALLYVAUGHAN

The O'Briens were the ruling dynasty of Munster. **Conor O'Brien** (d.1267) was King of Munster and is buried in an elaborate sculptured tomb in a recess in the Cistercian Abbey of Corcomroe, a few miles to the east of Ballyvaughan. His grandfather (also king of Munster), Domhnall O'Brien founded the abbey and is buried in St Mary's cathedral in Limerick.

Another O'Brien king, **Murtagh**, who died in 1120, is said, probably incorrectly, to be buried beneath a blocked-up Romanesque doorway in St Flannan's Church of Ireland Cathedral in Killaloe. In the same cathedral is an unusual thousand-year-old standing stone with ogham and runic writings. The inscriptions translate as "Thorgrimr carved this cross" and "A Blessing on Throgrimr" – perhaps a Viking who had converted to Christianity?

COORACLARE

The **Chevalier Thomas O'Gorman** (1732–1809), from Castletown, studied medicine at the Irish College in Paris and enlisted in the Irish Brigade, where his services were rewarded by his appointment as *chevalier* by King Louis XV. He married the daughter of a wine-maker from Burgundy, the Count d'Eon, inherited his estates and ran a successful wine export trade for many years between France and Ireland. On his business trips back to Ireland, he developed an interest in genealogy and began to compile family pedigrees for the expatriate Irish in France and Spain, many of whom were descendants of ancient Irish families. This proved to be a lucrative activity – for drawing up the pedigree of General Count Alexander O'Reilly in Spain he received a fee of one thousand guineas, no mean sum 200 years ago. These pedigrees were invaluable for expatriates seeking admission to court, marrying into titled French or Spanish families or securing promotions in the army.

O'Gorman became a noted collector of ancient Irish manuscripts and prevailed on the Irish College in Paris to return the *Book of Lecan* to the Royal Academy of Ireland.

Disaster struck in the form of the French Revolution when O'Gorman's extensive vineyards and estates were confiscated. He returned to Ireland, penniless, and settled in Dromellihy, near Cooraclare. He is buried in the old churchyard of Kilmacduane.

CORK

ABBEYSTREWERY ABBEY, SKIBBEREEN

One of the most moving graves to be seen anywhere in Ireland is the mass famine pit at Abbeystrewery on the outskirts of Skibbereen. It is estimated that between 8,000 and 10,000 bodies were interred in this plot during the Great Famine of the 1840s. The Workhouse and fever hospital records show that 5,000 deaths took place in Skibbereen alone but there were many more unrecorded deaths in the local houses and on the roadsides. Furthermore, many people buried their dead at night, ashamed that they could not afford a coffin or terrified to let it be known that the fever had affected their family. Lord Dufferin who visited the graveyard in Skibbereen in 1847 wrote:

the bodies had been daily thrown in, many without a coffin, one over another, the uppermost only hidden from the light of day by a bare three inches of earth, the survivors not even knowing the spot where those most dear to them lay sleeping.

The famine, the result of the repeated failure of the potato crop, was the greatest catastrophe to hit Ireland and changed it irrevocably, socially and politically. Even the landscape was changed as villages were deserted by famine victims and emigrants. Over 1,000,000 people died of starvation or of the many fevers which spread like wildfire through the famished and weakened population. Another 1,000,000 emigrated.

The workhouse in Skibbereen which in 1844 had housed fewer than 300 people was besieged by thousands of the "unfed, unclothed, unsheltered and unattended poor." Most had to be turned away. In any case, conditions inside the workhouse were so overcrowded that famine fever was endemic. Built to house 800, it frequently held thousands during the famine years.

Soup kitchens set up in Skibbereen supplied a meagre pint of soup daily to over 4,000 people in the Abbeystrewery district alone. People from the countryside around, many of them evicted from their small-holdings, flooded into the town, putting even greater pressure on those trying to provide some relief. The *Cork Examiner* reported that the prisons were crowded with "famine culprits, not one of whom when called up for trial was able to support himself in front of the dock".

The famine pit is now a large grassed-over area at the front of the cemetery. A small plaque commemorates the many people who are buried here and there is also an iron monument erected in 1887 to the memory of the famine victims by a local blacksmith.

ROSSCARBERY

One of the great heroes of the famine years was **Daniel Donovan** (1808–1877), the senior physician of the Skibbereen workhouse and an eloquent witness to the suffering of the time. Dr Donovan not only worked ceaselessly with the sick and the dying, raised collections, carried out inquests and organised the distribution of food, but also brought the scale of the disaster to the world's attention. He wrote countless articles to the local and London press and to medical journals describing in powerful and uncompromising language the tragedy that was unfolding. He helped organise free passage to England on empty cargo boats for emigrants, redeemed their pawned clothes and secured money to buy them food for the journey. He campaigned for improvements in the conditions in the prisons where overcrowding and poor rations made them a breeding-ground for fever and disease.

Dr Donovan survived the famine years but died blind and bedridden in 1877. He is buried in a large tomb overlooking the sea in the far right of the Abbey cemetery in Rosscarbery. The tomb does not mention him by name but is inscribed "the burying place of Dan Donovan who died in 1812 and his family", that is to say, the doctor's father. Epitaph or not, it is clear from every contemporary account that Donovan was a most admirable man. His obituary in the *Skibbereen and Cork County Journal* remarked: "When we consider what he must have endured in visiting the sick . . . entering sooty cabins, dens of pestilence, the inhabitants of which could not procure a candle, and, by the light of a splinter of bogwood, examining and prescribing for the destitute creatures stricken down by fever and pestilence – we, after a lapse of some years, are astounded how human nature was capable of such endurance."

(In many of the contemporary accounts of the famine, there is frequent mention of a sliding or hinged coffin or even starkly of "the parish coffin". This was a crude wooden box with a hinged base which could be used over and over again. A Doctor Thomas Willis, working in the Bantry area of West Cork during the famine years, was so moved by the use of the hinged coffin in his district, that he resolved it should never be buried or burned but be preserved as a memorial to those who perished during the famine years. He had three crucifixes made from the wood of the parish coffin. One of these he gave to the parish priest of Maynooth, Canon John O'Rourke, who later wrote an account of the famine years. This cross, the only one known to have survived, is now in the Presentation Convent, Maynooth in County Kildare.)

CREAGH

Although famine fever and dysentery mainly affected the

destitute and starving inhabitants of Skibbereen, it was by no means confined only to them. In Creagh churchyard, between Baltimore and Skibbereen on the seaward side of the road, lies the body of **Major Hugh Parker**, an English Commissioner of Relief. The stone on the table tomb tells us that he "died of a fever contracted in the execution of his duty on the relief service for the district of Skibbereen on 26 March 1847 aged (?) 36 years." Creagh churchyard is accessible by a grassy path which leads down from a gate on the main roadside. The church tower is just visible over a screen of high trees.

CASTLETOWNSHEND

The novelists **Edith Oenone Somerville** (1858–1949) and her first cousin **Violet Martin** (pen-name **Martin Ross**) (1862–1915) are buried side by side behind the lovely Church of St Barrohane in Castletownshend. Somerville's grave is marked by a large upright slab of local stone while Ross's is a cross with the inscription from the Book of Wisdom: "The Souls of the righteous are in the Land of God . . . in the sight of the unwise they seemed to die . . . but they are in peace."

After Ross's death, Somerville continued to "collaborate" with her and continued to name her as co-author of everything she published. They communicated with one another through a medium who took down what Ross "wrote". Their most popular work was a series of comic short stories, *Some Experiences of an Irish RM* (1908), about an English magistrate and his dealings with the devious and irascible native Irish.

In the porch of the church is an oar from one of the lifeboats of the Lusitania – many of the victims were washed ashore in the bay here (see Cobh).

FARAHY, NEAR KILDORRERY

Elizabeth Bowen, (1899–1973), one of the last novelists and short story writers in the Anglo-Irish tradition, died in

London but is buried near the front door of the church in Farahy, near Kildorrery, where the family home of Bowen's Court once stood.

Her novel *The Last September* is about the life of an Anglo-Irish household in Cork during the Troubles. The novel's focus is the big house itself and how it forms the characters of those who live in it. There are obvious parallels with her own home. Her ancestor, Lt. Col. Henry Bowen, had been granted the land after fighting in the Cromwellian army. In her book, *Bowen's Court*, she wrote: "A Bowen, in the first place, made Bowen's court. Since then, with a rather alarming sureness, Bowen's Court has made all the succeeding Bowens." She portrays the Ascendancy as irresponsible landlords of a country whose well-being they ignored, of old families entrenched in homes they could not afford to run, trying to ignore the sound of the rebellious Irish storming up the avenue. Towards the end of her life, unable to meet the running costs of the house, she sold Bowen's Court to a man who promptly demolished it. The key of the church is available from Molly O'Brien at her home opposite.

BALLYVOURNEY

Ballyvourney is in the Gaeltacht or Irish-speaking area in the heart of West Cork, west of Macroom. There is an ancient and rather strange graveyard here on the site where the local **Saint Gobnait** is supposed to be buried and which is now a shrine. Saint Gobnait (the name means honey bee) was a sixth-century abbess. She heard angels telling her she would "find her resurrection" where nine white deer grazed. The vision came true and she set up her abbey here. People still do "Stations" here, an ancient ritual which involves moving around saying special prayers at nine stations including Saint Gobnait's grave and a holy well under a tree which is bedecked with rosary beads and other offerings left by pilgrims.

In the newer part of the graveyard is the heather-covered grave of the musician and composer, **Sean Ó Riada** (1931–1971), who lived nearby in Coolea. Ó Riada revitalised Ireland's traditional musical heritage with his haunting musical score for the Gael Linn documentary, *Mise Éire*, in 1959. His group Ceoltóirí Cualann, a forerunner of The Chieftains, became immensely popular and influential in reawakening interest in Irish music. In addition to his many orchestral works, he wrote a Mass, originally commissioned for the monks of Glenstal Abbey, which uses traditional Irish instruments and is still sung by the all-male choir of the church at Coolea every Sunday. Ó Riada died tragically young at only forty years of age.

The poet Seán Ó Ríordáin (1916–1977) is buried in the same graveyard.

GOUGANEBARRA

Up in the remote and beautiful Gouganebarra Forest Park is another site of pilgrimage and the former home of anchorites. The name Gouganebarra means the "rock cleft of Finbarr", the saint who lived here as a hermit before founding the cathedral which bears his name in Cork city. Very little is known about Saint Finbarr and, according to the *Lives of the Irish Saints,* the little that is known "abounds in fables, some of which are so scandalous in character as to afford great disedification to pious readers." However, around the late 1600s, **Father Denis O'Mahony**, an eccentric and one of the last hermits in Ireland, came here to re-establish the site as a place of devotion to Saint Finbarr. He lived here on an island linked to the mainland by an artificial causeway in a reconstruction of Finbarr's cell. He soon became a tourist attraction in his own right, with speculation rife that he had been ordered there to do penance for "fornication". His tomb is on the side of the lake and became the centre of a cult for some time when pilgrims used to leave coins and votive offerings. Now only tourists and fishermen frequent this splendid place.

The lakeside of Gouganebarra is also the burial place of the famous story-teller, **Tim Buckley**, and his wife, **Ansty**, who held court in a nearby house on the road to the lake. Buckley's earthy humour attracted huge gatherings of neighbours and notables (including Frank O'Connor) and inspired Eric Cross (1903–1980) to write *The Tailor and Ansty,* a book deemed so bawdy and sacrilegious in the puritanical ethos of 1940s Ireland that it was banned.

CLOYNE

Sometimes a sport throws up an individual whose talent is so prodigious he acquires legendary status. The hurler **Christy Ring** (1920–1979) is one of those. At his graveside, the then Taoiseach Jack Lynch, himself no mean hurler, said of him: "as long as young boys swing their camans for the sheer tingle in their fingers of the impact of the ash with leather, as long as hurling is played, the story of Christy Ring will be told – and that will be forever."

It was not just that he won eight All-Ireland medals nor that he continued to play until well into his forties; Christy Ring was, by all accounts, a genius, an artist, a dazzling player without equal. He is buried in the Catholic Church graveyard in Cloyne in East Cork, by the wall on the right hand side: the tombstone just says "Ring". Opposite the church outside the Christy Ring Memorial Park, there is a striking statue of him by the sculptor Yann Goulet. The GAA stadium in Cork is also named after him.

COBH

Cobh, or Queenstown as it was once called, is one of the world's largest natural harbours and was the point of departure, not only for emigrant ships to America, but also for luxury transatlantic liners. On 7 May 1915, during the First

World War, the liner *Lusitania* was torpedoed by a German submarine off the coast of Cork with the loss of almost 1,200 lives. Many of the victims are buried in the Old Churchyard about a mile outside the town of Cobh. The graves, marked by a row of large boulders bearing the name of the ship, are located by the wall on the left of the main gate. Among those killed was **Sir Hugh Lane** (1875–1915), the art collector and nephew of Lady Gregory. In 1905 he had declared his intention to donate his collection to Dublin Corporation on condition they endowed a suitable gallery. When they failed to agree on the design for the gallery, he changed his mind and in 1913 drew up a new will bequeathing the paintings instead to the National Gallery in London. Shortly before he left for the United States on the *Lusitania*, he added a codicil to his will once again revoking this decision but his amended will was not witnessed. After a lengthy dispute a compromise was reached whereby the Hugh Lane Collection was divided and the two groups of paintings rotate between Dublin and London every five years. There is a monument to all the victims of the *Lusitania* in Casement Square on the sea-front near St Colman's Cathedral.

In a corner inside the ruined church in the old graveyard is the tomb of **Charles Wolfe** (1791–1823), the clergyman who wrote the ode "On the Burial of Sir John Moore". General Sir John Moore (1761–1809), who had helped quash the 1798 rebellion in Ireland and wrote an account of what he witnessed, was killed at Corunna during the Peninsular War and had to be buried clandestinely.

> *No useless coffin enclosed his breast*
> *Not in sheet or in shroud we wound him*
> *But he lay like a warrior taking his rest*
> *With his martial cloak around him*

The full poem, which is now displayed in a glass frame over Wolfe's tomb, first appeared in the *Newry Telegraph* in 1817. Charles Wolfe belonged to the family in Kildare from whom Theobald Wolfe Tone's grandfather rented a farm and Tone was named after one of the Wolfe family. I have heard it suggested that the poem may not refer to Moore's burial at all but to the equally clandestine burial of Wolfe Tone after his arrest and suicide in 1798. Charles Wolfe's own epitaph reads *The record of his genius/Piety and Virtue/Lives in the hearts/of all who knew him/Looking unto Jesus he lived/Looking unto Jesus he died/He is not dead but sleepeth.* He died of tuberculosis.

In keeping with Cobh's importance as a maritime centre, the Old Churchyard contains many more interesting tombs and graves which act as a reminder of how hazardous life aboard ship could be. Among the graves of master mariners, captains and admirals there are the remains of many deaths at sea. A memorial on the outside wall of the ruined church at the rear is for eighteen people who "died of a virulent dysentry which prevailed on board HMS Lapwing" in 1804. Another on the interior wall of the church is dedicated to the unfortunate writer and dramatist **John Tobin** (1769–1804) who, on the very day his ship was to set sail, "died at sea near the entrance of this harbour in the month of December 1804 on his passage to a milder climate in search of better health. Aged thirty-five." Only a few weeks later, *The Honey Moon,* his first successful play was premiered in London.

You can also see the tomb in a railed enclosure of **James Verling** (1787–1858) who, we are informed, was the official surgeon to Napoleon in St Helena in 1818–1819.

CORK

The English musician and composer, **Arnold Bax** (1883–1953) is buried in St Finbarr's Cemetery in Cork. In 1902, after reading Yeats' poem *The Wanderings of Oisin*, he wrote in his entertaining memoirs, "in a moment the Celt within me stood revealed. I knew that I too must follow Oisin and Niamh into the sunset". He moved to Ireland, learned

Irish, studied history and folklore and even adopted an Irish alter ego, **Dermot O'Byrne**. Under this pen-name he wrote several novels and poems, one of which in commemoration of the 1916 Rising was banned as seditious. His Celtic transformation was so convincing that his friend George Russell (AE) once sent him a press cutting which authoritatively declared that Arnold Bax was a pseudonym used for musical purposes by a West of Ireland poet called Dermot O'Byrne! Arnold Bax was the composer of seven symphonies as well as chamber music. He was knighted in 1937 and appointed Master of the King's Music in 1942.

Francis Sylvester Mahony (1804–1866), is buried in the churchyard in the Mahony family tomb in St Ann's Church, better known as the Shandon Church on the hill north of the river Lee. A Jesuit, he gave up the priesthood and moved to London where he wrote for *Fraser's Magazine* under the pseudonym Father Prout and later to Paris where he was correspondent for the *Globe*. *The Shandon Bells*, his verses on the landmark church of St Ann, have made the church a tourist attraction where visitors for a small fee can have a go at ringing the bells.

The dramatist and short story writer, **Daniel Corkery** (1878–1964) is buried in St Joseph's Cemetery in Turner's Cross, Cork. His book, *The Hidden Ireland* (1924), is a celebration of the lyric poets and Courts of poetry in Munster of the eighteenth century and a controversial account of how "the soul of the Gael" is revealed in Irish poetry. He declared that any history of Ireland which did not take into account the importance of Irish and its literature was flawed and incomplete. He wrote "The Ascendancy's creed is, and always has been, that the natives are a lesser breed, and that anything that is theirs (except their land and their gold) is therefore of little value."

As a teacher in Cork, he taught and inspired both Frank O'Connor and Sean Ó Faolain. He later became professor of English at University College Cork.

Corkery's grave is inside the main gate of the cemetery on the left hand side, the headstone simply inscribed with his name in Irish.

KILCREA

Off the road between Cork and Macroom are the ancient ruins of Kilcrea Franciscan Abbey. Here in a railed off corner of the chapel is the tomb of **Art O'Leary,** the subject of one of the most famous Gaelic poems, *Caoineadh Airt Ui Laoghaire (The Lament for Art O'Leary).* His epitaph reads:

> *Lo; Arthur Leary, generous, handsome, brave*
> *Slain in his bloom, lies in this humble grave*
> *Died 4th May 1773, Aged 26 years.*

Art was a handsome fiery-tempered young man who had served with the Hungarian Hussars. On his return to Ireland he married a young widow, **Eibhlin Dubh Ni Chonaill** (c.1743–1800), one of twenty-two children of Daniel O'Connell's grandfather. At the Macroom Races in 1773, Art O Leary's horse outran the horse of an old adversary, Abraham Morris. Morris invoked a law which decreed that a Protestant, under certain circumstances, could buy the horse of any Catholic – no matter how valuable – for five pounds. They came to blows and O'Leary had to go on the run. Some months later, he set out to ambush Morris but he himself was killed. The riderless and bloodied horse raced home to Eibhlin Dubh, but, by the time she arrived at her husband's side, O'Leary was already dead. Lying over his body, she cups her palm, drinks his still-flowing blood, and begins to compose her lament. It is a very fine poem, full of pain and remorse and, indeed, her determination for revenge.

> *Till Art O Leary rise*
> *This grief will never yield*
> *That's bruising all my heart*
> *Yet shut up fast in it*
> *As Twere in a locked trunk*

> *with the key gone astray*
> *and rust grown on the wards.*

(Translation Frank O'Connor)

The abbey has been the site of burials since its foundation. In the north-eastern corner of the choir is the grave of the founder of the abbey, a Munster chieftain, Lord of Muskerry and builder of Blarney Castle, **Cormac Laidir McCarthy**, (d.1465). Directly opposite, on the ground, is a recently placed plaque commemorating a bishop, **Tomás Sar Oirmidneac**, who attended the third session of the Council of Trent in 1562–3, the council convened by the Pope to strengthen the Church's opposition to the spread of Protestantism and which defined the doctrine of transubstantiation.

Kilcrea Abbey may appear to be rather neglected now but it is not as gruesome as it was when Mr and Mrs Hall paid a visit to it in the 1840s. In their account of their journey around Ireland, they wrote: "As in all ancient churches, human bones are piled in every nook and cranny, thrust into corners, or gathered in heaps directly at the entrance – a sight far more revolting than effecting . . . " Even so, they noted that a "picnic party were regaling" in the transept.

In 1895 when the Secretary of Cork Historical and Archaeological Society inspected the abbey, it was still "deplorable, so overcrowded that a gravedigger usually has to penetrate through and throw aside the remains of other coffins. The ground has been so raised by burials it has reached the arches at the top of the doorways." After some work was carried out, an inspector in 1897 found the situation hardly improved. "The condition of the graveyard is impossible to describe – coffins over ground, corpses hardly covered . . . it is positively dangerous to send workmen there. The practice of placing a coffin only about eighteen inches below the level of the ground and then raising a mound of earth over it still continues."

Be assured the visitor will find nothing as off-putting today.

GLANDORE

The fate of the body of **William Thompson** (1785–1833) is unclear but I hope I will be forgiven in including him here even though he no longer has a grave! Thompson was an extraordinary man whose political ideas were years ahead of his time and are said to have been an influence on Karl Marx. (There is even a statue of him in the International Communist Museum in Prague.)

Thompson owned large tracts of land near Glandore where, much to the displeasure of his family, he set up a pioneer cooperative estate. A teetotaller, vegetarian, non-smoking, militant anti-cleric, he must have been a rather singular resident of the area at the time. On his death he was buried in Drombeg cemetery but then, when his will was read, he was found to have left instructions that "no priest, Christian, Mohammedan or Hindu" should have anything to do with his remains. Instead, he wanted his body to be preserved and put on display, the ribs tipped with silver, to discourage "the prejudice against the public examination of corpses." The final destination of the body is unknown but the skull ended up in the hands of a French phrenologist. A Doctor Donovan, presumably the same doctor from Skibbereen mentioned earlier in connection with the famine, was instructed to send the bones as a memento to a Mrs Wheeler, a proponent of female emancipation, but whether she received them – or would have welcomed them – I cannot say.

BLARNEY

A pioneering Cork doctor, **Richard Barter** (1802–1870), is buried in the old churchyard at Innishannon. During the 1832 cholera epidemic Barter became convinced of the curative power of water and subsequently established the St Anne's water cure at his home about a mile outside Blarney. It rapidly expanded and attracted visitors from all over the world, seeking relief from their rheumatism, bronchial trouble and skin diseases. He then invited the orientalist David Urquhart to come to Blarney to set up what became the first Turkish baths in the British Isles. The establishment went on to become one of the biggest employers in the Cork area. Subsequently, under Dr Barter's direction, many more Irish cities and towns opened public baths and hot rooms and Turkish baths were installed in the larger hospitals.

In recent years, the Innishannon graveyard had become very neglected and two sycamore trees had grown out of the Barter tomb, breaking it open in places. Although the site has now been cleared and restored, the Barter name has disappeared, a sad instance of how the memorials of the dead are lost. However, it is worth looking for the Huguenot graves here. Innishannon was once home to a community of Huguenots who set up a weaving industry here and even planted a mulberry orchard for the production of silk.

KILCRUMPER

Tis of a famous highwayman a story I will tell
His name was Willy Brennan and in Ireland he did dwell
Twas on the Kilworth mountain he commenced his wild career
where many a gallant gentleman before him shook with fear.

The outlaw and popular hero of the ballad "Brennan on the Moor" was a Waterford man but carried out most of his exploits in County Tipperary. Eventually he was captured – betrayed they say by a comrade for the price on his head – and executed in Clonmel Gaol. He was buried in Kilcrumper, midway between Kilworth and Fermoy. His grave is not marked but is traditionally pointed out beneath a niche in the only wall now standing of the ruined church.

KERRY

BLENNERVILLE

Despite Dublin's claim to be the final burying-place of the executed body of the United Irishman, **Robert Emmet** (1778–1803), there is an intriguing case to be made for Blennerville, near Killarney, where Emmet's mother was born. This is a story whose ingredients include a headless corpse, a secret society, a murder, a cover-up and a team of diviners.

The plot begins thirty odd years ago when an Australian priest wrote to the parish priest at Blennerville for help in tracing information about the murder of an ancestor of his called Kearney. The research threw up an interesting local story about Robert Emmet.

A haulage contractor, Patrick MacMahon from Tralee, had a contract to remove garbage from the prison where Emmet was held. Soon after his execution, an artist took Emmet's severed head away to make a death mask (which incidentally is on display at St Michan's church in Dublin) but when he returned it to the jail, the rest of the body had already been disposed of.

Local tradition in Kerry was that MacMahon had been paid to smuggle Emmet's body out of the prison and have it sent on to Kerry for burial, possibly at Castlemaine where Emmet's grandmother is buried. The convoy was stopped at Headley's Bridge by the local Whiteboys who took the box containing the headless corpse, unaware of its contents. When MacMahon heard what had happened, he went to see the leader of the Whiteboys, Kearney, in order to retrieve the body. However, fearing that he had been followed, he shot Kearney to stop him revealing what he knew to the authorities. (This Kearney was the ancestor of the Australian priest whose enquiries had provoked the investigation.) Emmet's body was then supposed to have been secretly buried at night in the churchyard at Blennerville.

In 1965, three diviners were employed to try to locate the remains and establish the truth of the tradition. One, Dr Pierce, from Listowel, working with a photograph, the death mask and a penknife, got a pull from Dublin but it turned out to be the grave of the artist who had made the mask! However the other two diviners, Shanahan and McCarthy both independently divined Emmet's body at Blennnerville and the head in Ringsend, Dublin.

The area around the church porch was then dug up and the remains of a grave were found though whether it had ever contained Emmet's headless body, who can tell? The enigma of Robert Emmet's grave must remain unanswered. The murdered Whiteboy, Kearney, is also believed to be buried in the same churchyard.

The ground has since been taken over by the Urban District council and is now known as the Robert Emmet Park.

DINGLE

Peig Sayers (1873–1958) is buried on a cliff-top in the new cemetery of Dunquin in view of the Great Blasket island where she had lived for forty years. One of the Irish-speaking writers from the Blaskets, Peig was renowned as a story-teller and was the first woman to write about the Gaeltacht from a woman's perspective in her autobiography, *Peig*. A native of Dunquin, Peig had married a Blasket islander, "Pats Flint", in an arranged marriage. Her home on the island was soon a focus for all the islanders where she would hold court discoursing on this and that and re-telling the old myths and legends. The Irish Folklore Commission took down hundreds of stories from her – it was widely believed that if all the old legends of Ireland had been lost, Peig could have recalled them all. She was one of the last inhabitants of the island, surviving long after her husband's death and the emigration of all her children. In *An Old Woman Remembers* she wrote of her own death: "People will yet walk into the graveyard where I am lying – I'll be stretched out there quietly and the old world will have vanished." As indeed it has: the Blasket community was evacuated from the islands in 1953.

Peig was just one of several renowned writers from the Blaskets. **Tomás Ó Criomhthain** (1856–1937), the author of *An t-Oileánach (The Islandman)* is buried in the old Dunquin cemetery. Unlike Peig he was born and bred on the island and his account of life off-shore is a harsher, less romantic one, mostly concerned with the dangers, the hardships and the isolation that islanders had to endure.

It is perhaps worth pointing out that Blasket islanders were usually buried on the mainland in or around Dunquin even when the island community was quite large. The small graveyard on the island was used only for unbaptised babies, victims of shipwrecks or suicides. In the end, it was a delay in getting a coffin to the mainland because of bad weather that finally convinced the islanders to leave for good.

SNEEM

In 1976 **Cearbhall Ó Dálaigh** (1911–1978) resigned as President of Ireland after only two years in office. In September of that year he had referred an Emergency Powers Bill to the Supreme Court to test its constitutionality. (He had been a former Chief Justice for Ireland.) The court ruled that the bill was constitutional but, meanwhile, the Minister of Defence had called the President "a thundering disgrace".

When no apology was forthcoming, Ó Dalaigh resigned to "assert publicly my personal integrity and independence as President of Ireland and to protect the dignity and independence of the presidency as an institution." He then retired to live in the pretty village of Sneem where he died less than two years later. He is buried on the left hand side of the main pathway in Sneem graveyard. The memorial, a large horizontal stone, carries his name and the inscription in Latin: "I have chosen the way of truth: and thy judgements have I laid before me."

If you see a small marble panda incongruously sitting on a rock on Quay Road, that too is another memorial to President O Dálaigh. It was presented by the Chinese People's Association for Friendship with Foreign Countries and dedicated to the memory of the first Irish president to visit China.

MUCKROSS

There are three Gaelic poets buried in the grounds of Muckross Abbey, now part of the Muckross national park, near Killarney. All of them were colourful characters who have been described by the writer Kate O'Brien as "almost to a man, rakes, drinkers, woman leavers and priest-cursers."

The poet, **Eoghan Ruadh Ó Súilleabháin**, (1748–1784) was killed by servants of a Colonel Cronin in a row over a poem that Eoghan Ruadh had dedicated to him. In the course of the fight, he was badly concussed and became feverish. He might have recovered but for his love of drink. While still convalescing, he went on a drinking binge which caused a relapse. On the night he was to be buried, a storm prevented the burial party from crossing the river so a temporary and unmarked grave was dug. Later he may have been re-interred in the Abbey with his family.

There is a memorial to him and to the other Kerry Poets, **Aodhagan O'Rahilly** (d.1728), **Geoffrey O'Donoghue** (d.1677) and **Pierce Ferriter** (d.1653) at Muckross and another at Martyr's Hill, Killarney. Pierce Ferriter, a chieftain of Dingle and of Norman descent, was renowned as a composer of courtly love poems. He was hanged at this spot in Killarney for his part in the 1641 rebellion. The memorial, sculpted by Seamus Murphy, is of a spéir-bhean ("sky-woman"), a vision of Ireland celebrated in the aisling or dream poems.

Rudolph Eric Raspe (1737–1794) was a German mining engineer and author of a book of hyperbolic adventure tales, *Baron Munchausen's Narrative of his Marvellous Travels and Campaigns in Russia,* which purports to be a true account of the adventures of a German soldier and raconteur. Unfortunately, Raspe did not confine his yarn-spinning to literature. He had come to Ireland to escape the wrath of a Scottish landowner whom he had deceived into thinking his land was rich in ore and made off with his reward before the truth was known. In his new position as manager of the Killarney copper mines, he was probably intending to pull off a similar scam but caught typhoid fever and died at Muckross. He is buried somewhere in the small burial ground overlooking the Killarney lakes.

FOLEY'S GLEN, NEAR TRALEE

Many early Christian ogham stones, beehive huts, inscribed crosses and ancient grave slabs are to be found all over Kerry and its off-shore islands. In the area known as Foley's Glen in the mountains about three miles south of Tralee, there is a large natural boulder which is supposed to be the burial place of **Scota**, a Pharaoh's daughter and the wife of the Spanish King Meliseus. She had come to Ireland with her sons and died in battle near Sliabh Mis. The ogham inscription which translates as "the grave-mound of Scoithin" was probably added some time in the nineteenth century.

LIMERICK

LIMERICK

St Mary's Church of Ireland Cathedral stands on King's Island in the Shannon estuary on a bedrock of Limerick limestone. In the graveyard there is a striking example of a tall Celtic cross carved in this limestone. In autumn it stands out against a magnificent back-drop of Burgundy-coloured Virginia creeper. This is the grave of **Charles Graves** (1812–1899) , father of AP Graves and grandfather of the poet Robert Graves. Charles Graves was Bishop of Limerick for thirty-three years, the last Bishop of the Established Church of Ireland. An eminent mathematician and Gaelic scholar, he led the commission which translated the Brehon Laws into English and made many transcriptions of ancient ogham writings.

Writing about his experiences as a British soldier stationed in Limerick in 1919, "a foreign enemy to the city with which my family had been connected for over two hundred years", the bishop's grandson, the poet Robert Graves, recalls being told by an old antique dealer that the Catholic bishop had made attendance at his grandfather's wake compulsory as a tribute to Bishop Graves' eminence as a Gaelic scholar. His scholarship was not confined to Gaelic. In his son AP Graves's autobiography, *To Return to All That,* we read that his father was so "fine and well-grounded a scholar that he was able to converse freely in Latin with one of the brothers Grimm whom he met while travelling on the continent."

The Celtic cross was erected by Bishop Graves's family who had all left Ireland by the time of his death. It has inscriptions in Latin, English and Irish, the Irish one written by Douglas Hyde, later to become the first president of Ireland.

On a pillar inside the cathedral there is a tablet memorial to one of the first Barringtons of Limerick, **Samuel Barrington**, the clock-maker, whose quirky epitaph reads:

> *Memento mory.*
> *Here lieth littell Samuell*
> *Barinton that great under*
> *taker of famous cittis*
> *clock and chime maker*
> *He made his one time goe*
> *early and latter but now*
> *he is returned to God his creator:*
> *the 19 of November then he*
> *scest and for his memory*
> *this here is pleast by his*
> *son Ben. 1693."*

The Barringtons had probably come to Ireland with Cromwell. They became the leading merchants of Limerick, founded the first public hospital there and established a charitable pawnshop, the Mont de Piété, the first in the British Isles. Many of them are buried in the cathedral, including the first of the family to settle in the city, **Sir Francis Barrington** (d. 1693). Their home, Glenstal Castle, was given to the state in 1925 and now houses the Benedictine Abbey and Glenstal school. (See also the entry for Abington cemetery where Winifred Barrington, murdered in 1921, is buried.)

The tomb of **Murrogh O'Brien, Lord Inchiquin** (1614–1674), is near the baptistery on the north aisle of the cathedral, though whether he still lies within is debatable since tradition has it that his body was dug up the day after his burial by the enraged citizens of Limerick who stormed into the cathedral and flung him into the Shannon. During the Confederate Wars of the 1640s, Lord Inchiquin was appointed president of Munster by the English parliament. He fought against the Irish confederates, expelled nearly all the Roman Catholics from Cork, Youghal and Kinsale and gained notoriety as Murchadh na dtoiteán (" Murrough, the burner of churches"). He even set fire to the Rock of Cashel, piling turf on the wooden structures and massacring the garrison within. After Cromwell's arrival in Ireland in 1649, Inchiquin's power diminished. He removed himself to France where he joined the court of Charles II and, expediently, became a Roman Catholic himself.

Michael Hogan (1832–1899), the bard of Thomond, was renowned for his scurrilous and satirical lays and verse. One of the best known is "Drunken Thady and the Bishop's Lady" which still has resonance.

> *"Tis true she lived – tis true she died*
> *Tis true she was a Bishop's bride:*
> *But for herself tis little matter*
> *To whom she had been wife or daughter."*

Such is the fate of women who get involved with bishops. Hogan is buried near the entrance of the principal municipal cemetery in Limerick, Mount St Laurence. Unfortunately the original memorial, a Celtic cross, was destroyed by vandals in 1986. A public subscription was launched to raise a new monument and this is now in place, hopefully to be left in peace.

Michael Hogan worked for some time for the merchant **Thompson Russell** whom he dismissed in verse as "Tuppenny Tom". Thompson Russell (d.1880), the managing director of the vast Russell Mills, is buried in the family crypt in St John's graveyard in St John's Square. He was no stranger to the interior of the tomb during his own lifetime. Whether he had a death wish or merely wanted to be left in peace, Russell had the crypt fitted out with a desk, chair, lamp and stove, and spent many evenings working alone inside it until eventually he was in no position to leave. Russell's tomb is surely unique in that it shares a party wall with a pub, The Holy Ground – the only pub in Ireland situated within the precincts of a graveyard. As the American poet, Knute Skinner, commented

this pub houses the quick and the dead
And those who mark time
in the snug bar tipple by the bones . . .

An old plaque with a Latin inscription on the outer wall of this graveyard records that the walls were badly damaged during the Siege of Limerick and that the parishioners had them rebuilt at their own expense in 1693. A new plaque with an English translation has recently been erected alongside it.

KILMURRY

Time and weather obliterate epitaphs; even gravestones themselves are buried. During recent renovation and clearing of the Kilmurry graveyard on the outskirts of Limerick, an old stone was uncovered and its history rediscovered. After Lord Edward Fitzgerald was betrayed and killed in Dublin in 1798, his wife, Pamela, a French noblewoman, was banished from Ireland with her three small children. One of her daughters, also Pamela, returned to Ireland when she married Lt. Col. Sir Guy Campbell – they lived at Plassey House in Limerick for some time in the 1820s. The gravestone that was found in Kilmurry marked the grave of their infant son, **John Campbell**, who died in 1828. The horizontal slab had sunk beneath the turf but has now been cleaned, re-incised and replaced but there is nothing to indicate to the casual grave-spotter that John's family background was so illustrious. His grandfather, Lord Edward Fitzgerald, was interred in a vault in St Werburgh's Church in Dublin after his execution. His mother, Lady Campbell, is buried in England where Lord Edward's wife Pamela was also re-interred. She had died in Paris in 1831 and was buried in Montmartre. During the Siege of Paris in 1870 her monument was damaged by Prussian shelling. Some years later her remains were about to be placed in the Fosse Commune but were rescued by an Irish man of letters, JP Leonard, who visited Montmartre on his Grand Tour. He took Lady Pamela's remains back to England for reburial with her daughter.

KILEELY

The pioneer doctor and surgeon, **Sylvester O'Halloran** (1728–1807) was one of many Irishmen who, denied the opportunities of education in Ireland because of the penal laws, went overseas to study. He studied medicine in London, Leyden and Paris and returned to practice in his home city of Limerick in 1749 where he cut a striking and elegant figure, according to a contemporary account, "in his quaint French dress, with his gold-headed cane, beautiful Parisian wig and cocked hat."

O'Halloran pioneered the treatment of glaucoma and cataracts and made innovative surgical advances in amputation and head injuries. Indeed, his *Treatise on Injuries of the Head* published in 1793 conjures up an interesting picture of the Irish society of his day:

> *There is no part of the habitable globe, that for half a century past, has afforded such an ample field for observation on injuries of the head, as Ireland in general; this province of Munster in particular! For our people, invincibly brave, notwithstanding the cruel oppressions they have suffered for a century past, and highly irritable, soon catch fire: a slight offence is frequently followed by serious consequences; and sticks, stones, and every other species of offence next to hand, are dealt out with great liberality! To this add the frequent abuse of spirituous liquors, particularly whiskey, which has, unhappily for the morals and constitutions of the people, found its way to every part of the kingdom.*

In between trepanning skulls, O'Halloran found time to found Limerick's first public hospital and first "lying-in" hospital for women, published a history of Ireland, was active in public affairs and became widely known as an antiquarian. He is buried in the family vault in Kileely cemetery. This little walled cemetery, surrounded over the years by Corporation houses, had become very neglected and overgrown but was restored about twenty years ago when the vault was rediscovered and a new memorial erected to "Sylvester O'Halloran . . . historian, surgeon, antiquary, patriot."

ABINGTON

On 16 May 1921, at Coolboreen bridge, the IRA ambushed District Inspector Henry Biggs, killing him and his companion, a young lady called **Winifred Barrington** (1898–1921) whose family had had associations with Limerick for over 300 years. Winifred, a nurse with the Voluntary Ambulance Division during the First World War, had been with a fishing party which included District Inspector Biggs, an allegedly ruthless Black and Tan officer. On their return journey, their motor car was attacked by a local IRA brigade. Biggs was shot dead instantly. Miss Barrington fell into the ditch. The IRA then approached the car as Sean Gaynor, one of the ambush party describes: "McGrath, Ryan and myself then went up to the car, where we found, unharmed, an English woman named Rivers. She was by no means frightened, and proceeded to give us 'dog's abuse' for having shot Miss Barrington. *Miss River's language upset me somewhat, but Ryan quickly silenced her when he said 'Only for the bitch being in bad company she would not be shot.'*" (My italics). She died a few hours later.

Winifred Barrington was buried in the cemetery at Abington, near Glenstal. Her headstone reads poignantly:

here lies
all that could die of

Winifred Frances Barrington
loved and only daughter of
Sir Charles B. Barrington Bt.
Of Glenstal
The Barringtons left Glenstal and Ireland shortly afterwards.

GLIN

Just outside Glin, in the churchyard of Kilfergus, the stonecutter Tim Costello's family have erected a truly original headstone over his grave. The epitaph is almost certainly the work of the bard of Thomond, Michael Hogan. **Timothy Costello** died in June 1873 aged 85.

> *This is the grave of Tim Costello*
> *Who lived and died a right good fellow*
> *From his boyhood to life's end*
> *he was the poor man's faithful friend.*
> *He fawn'd before no purse-proud clod*
> *He fear'd none but the living God*
> *and never did he do to others*
> *but what was right to do to brothers.*
> *He loved green Ireland's mountains bold*
> *her verdant vales and abbeys old*
> *He loved her music, song and story*
> *He wept for her long blighted glory*
> *And often did I hear him pray*
> *that God would end her spoilers sway*
> *To men like him may peace be given*
> *In this world and in heaven. Amen.*

At the top of the headstone is a wonderful carving of what looks like a ceilidh in Heaven. The "craic" looks mighty. A general air of communal good humour, wine and song prevails with a cheerful bearded God, an embracing couple and a kneeling child attentively listening to a group of musicians playing the lyre and the harp. It is certainly more encouraging that a skull and cross-bones.

Kilfergus graveyard is also the burial place of the **Knights of Glin**, all but six of whom were buried in the vault here between 1400–1866. The Knights of Glin were a branch of the Fitzgeralds, the title being first documented in 1425 when John fitz John Fitzgerald became the first Knight of Glin. Since then they have been colourfully and inextricably linked with the history, legends, poetry and folklore of Limerick.

CROOM

The origin of the Limerick is attributed to a group of poets who lived in the area around the river Maigue in the eighteenth century. One of these, **Sean Ó Tuama** (1706–1775), is buried in the Church of Ireland graveyard in Croom, opposite the Croom mill. For some time Ó Tuama had kept an inn at Mungret Gate in the city of Limerick but ended up looking after hens for the formidable Mrs Windham Quin of Adare manor – and no wonder if he was as generous as he claimed:

> *No landless wanderer of the noble Gael*
> *Nor brother bard, no doughty heart and game*
> *Though presently he lack the price of ale,*
> *but John O Twomey welcomes all the same.*

One of his "brother bards", **Aindrias MacCraith**, or Andrew McGrath (d. 1795), is buried against the wall of the Collegiate Church of St Saviour in the old town of Kilmallock (*not* in the priory which is adjacent and which was one of the monasteries burned down by the infamous Murrough O'Brien – see Limerick.) Mac Craith sometimes worked as a hedge schoolmaster but was more widely known as An Mangaire Súgach ("the Jolly Pedlar"). Like his friend Sean Ó Tuama he clearly enjoyed a drink. In one of his poems he writes:

> *is maith an bheart i n-aon*
> *Do chaith a choróinn 's a réal,*
> *'s a liacht scramaire gan chéill*
> *Do mealladh ris an saoghal*

Atá anois ag dreoghadh san chré
Fir ag a mnáibh dá n'éis
Is iad-san fá líg san teampull.

(It's a good thing for a man to spend his crown, his shilling, considering how many people now rot beneath the clay, their wives with new men, and they under a stone in the cemetery.)

I hope he felt he had had enough to drink for now he is under a stone in the cemetery. The monument over his grave was erected in 1970 by Tomás Ó Fiaich (later Cardinal and Archbishop of Armagh).

FOYNES

Outside the Flying Boat museum in the square in Foynes (Foynes was the precursor of Shannon International Airport – the first international flights to America took off and landed on the waters here) there is a monument in honour of **Stephen de Vere** (1812–1904), the Limerick landowner and brother of the poet Aubrey de Vere. Stephen de Vere was a tireless campaigner for improved conditions on the emigrant ships to North America. Hundreds of thousands of Irish people set off for a new life in America in the aftermath of the famine – 215,000 in the year 1847 alone – though many did not survive the atrocious journey on the so-called coffin ships. Overcrowding, filthy conditions, lice, poor rations and the lack of clean drinking water, exacerbated by the poor health of the emigrants to begin with, made the ships a natural breeding ground for disease. In April 1847, Stephen de Vere travelled steerage with a group of emigrants from Limerick to see the conditions for himself.

He described the journey: "hundreds of poor people, men, women and children, huddled together, without light, without air, wallowing in filth and breathing a fetid atmosphere, sick in body, dispirited in heart; the fevered patients lying between the sound, in sleeping places so narrow as almost to deny them . . . a change of position; living without food or medicine except as administered by the hand of casual charity. . . . no cleanliness was enforced; the beds never aired; the master during the whole voyage never entered the steerage, and would listen to no complaints; false measures were used (in which the water and several articles of dry food were served), the gallon measure containing but three quarts, which fact I proved in Quebec, and had the captain fined for; lights were prohibited, because the ship with her open fire-grates upon deck, was freighted with Government powder for the garrison of Quebec . . . "

De Vere's subsequent report, read out in Parliament, made such a profound impression that many of his recommendations for reform were accepted. Legislation to regulate conditions at sea and the reception and quarantine of passengers on their arrival in Canada followed. De Vere himself rented a large house in Quebec where those emigrants whose passage he had paid could shelter and recover from the effects of their journey before looking for work. He returned to Ireland in the autumn of 1848 and is buried in Mount Trenchard graveyard (between Foynes and Glin).

ASKEATON

Stephen's brother, **Aubrey de Vere** (1814–1902), the poet and landowner of the Curragh Chase demesne, is buried in the churchyard in Askeaton, on the left hand side just inside the gate. Aubrey de Vere was an exemplary landlord during the famine years and at the forefront in the setting up of relief programmes for tenants. He converted to Catholicism in 1851.

KNOCKPATRICK

High up on the hill of Knockpatrick overlooking Foynes is the grave of **Charlotte Grace O'Brien** (1845–1909), the poet and daughter of the Young Ireland leader, William Smith O'Brien. Her grave, marked by a horizontal headstone with beautiful filigree carvings, lies outside the wall of the ruined church on the river side commanding spectacular views of the whole Shannon estuary and islands. The graveyard is accessible through a gate on the main road over farmland – the last part of the climb must be undertaken on foot.

Charlotte Grace O'Brien, like her friend Stephen de Vere, also campaigned about conditions on the emigrant "coffin ships" to America. At the age of thirty-five, profoundly deaf and without family ties, she re-launched her life as an activist for emigrant Irishwomen. Appalled by the plight of emigrants, both at sea and on land awaiting passage, she established and ran a 105-bed boarding-house for young women and girls in Cobh. She visited the ships every morning with a medical officer to lobby for the improvement and enforcement of safety and health regulations, and the provision of separate berths for single and married people. In 1882 she travelled to New York herself (though making the journey as a non-steerage passenger) where she lived in a tenement house to see for herself the impact of emigration on the "innumerable unprotected girls who were swarming through my own hands in Queenstown".

Her missionary work did not escape criticism. The Fenian, John Boyle O'Reilly, railed against emigration as a social evil to be condemned; in his opinion, easing the conditions of emigrants avoided the main issues of land reform in Ireland. In January 1883 in the *Boston Pilot* he wrote "let the odium for their (condition) fall on the shoulders of the English government . . . and let their death protest against the merciless hand that drives them out of their own land . . . " Charlotte Grace O'Brien pragmatically and in a more humanitarian spirit responded:

" . . . I cannot close my eyes to the fact that a large part of Ireland is in deep distress; that starvation is in parts imminent, that the steamships companies have lowered their fares, and that in America there is fair prosperity, that these circumstances combined will produce a heavy immigration . . . no declamation will prevent it."

Charlotte's father, **William Smith O'Brien**, (1803–1864), of Dromoland Castle, was a former MP for Ennis who had joined the Young Ireland movement. Charlotte would scarcely have known him since she was only three years old when he took part in the ill-planned and abortive Fenian rising at Ballingarry, County Tipperary in 1848 and was transported to Tasmania. He returned to Ireland in 1856 but took no further part in political life. He died in Bangor in Wales.

TIPPERARY

Richard Crosbie (b. 1755) from Wicklow, was Ireland's first aeronaut, making the first manned balloon ascent from the newly-opened pleasure gardens at Ranelagh in Dublin in 1783. This was in the pioneering days of flying when the Montgolfier Brothers were making the first free balloon ascents in France. Many of these experiments ended disastrously as a memorial to Cadman, an early English "flying man", outside St Mary's Church in Shrewsbury records:

> Let this small monument record the name
> Of Cadman, and to future times proclaim
> How by'n attempt to fly from this high spire
> Across the Sabrine stream he did acquire
> His fatal end. Twas not for want of skill
> Or courage to perform the task he fell:
> No, no, a faulty cord being drawn too tight
> Hurried his soul on high to take her flight,
> Which bid his body here below, Good Night.

The inventive agent for the Lismore Estate, **Henry Eeles** (d.1781), took out a patent on a "flying coach" or steerable balloon about 1750 and it is said that he took it on exhibition flights over Tipperary and the coast of Waterford. This would make him the unsung pioneer of manned flight but evidence that his flying coach ever took off the ground is hard to come by! However, his experiments in electrotherapy and renown as an "electric doctor" providing electrical remedies for "agues and palsies" for a large and grateful clientele are better documented. He used to conduct experiments with kites during lightning storms on the Knockmealdown mountains and wrote learned papers on the "Cause of Thunder" for the Royal Society. So, appropriately enough, it was there, on the very summit of the Sugarloaf, that he requested to be buried.

Mr Eeles' funeral on the mountain side lasted many days, with "mourners" overnighting in tents at the foot of the mountain and heroic quantities of poteen being consumed. It was widely believed at the time that he had been buried with his horse and hounds though it seems unlikely that his menagerie would have been slaughtered on his death. There were also suggestions that an iron rod had been driven through his body to attract lightning.

The landowner, **Samuel Grubb** (1855–1921) also opted to be buried in an unusual site high up above the Vee road near Clogheen. At his request, he was buried standing bolt upright in a stone beehive-shaped cairn built of white masonry, the better to watch over his home, Castlegrace House, in the valley below.

BOHERLAHAN

Charles Bianconi (1786–1875) was the Italian who set up the first "car" service in Ireland, carrying passengers and goods between Clonmel and Cahir in 1815. After a slow start, business boomed and soon Bianconi's fleet of forty-five cars were travelling over 3,600 miles every day. Each car held between four and sixteen passengers who paid one or two pence per mile, depending on the number of turnpikes on the road and whether they sat inside or outside. Bianconi's fortune was made. He also set up a coach factory at Clonmel to build and repair his cars.

The business had a considerable impact on rural life, opening up all sorts of business and social opportunities. Hitherto unavailable goods and merchandise reached every corner of the country. But its greatest boon was to the feet of the Irish. Suddenly, for the price of a few shillings, a man could complete a round trip of, say, sixty miles and carry out a few hours business in one day, an outing that previously would have taken three days.

Bianconi sold his business on his retirement in 1865 to his agents and employees, but by then, the railways were already superseding the car service. He is buried beside the Catholic church at Boherlahan – the family vault is an enormous monument in the style of a Romanesque chapel.

CASHEL

As you drive towards Cashel the great Rock of Cashel rises dramatically into view. This was the seat of royal and ecclesiatiacal power from the fifth century until 1647 when it was finally destroyed by Cromwell's army. The notorious apostate Bishop Magrath, "The Scoundrel of Cashel" is buried on the Rock, in the choir on the right hand side of the cathedral.

If there is any truth in the remark that "the good die young" then it is apt that the archbishop, **Meiler** or **Myler Magrath** (1523–1622), died just short of his hundredth birthday. A devious, malign and rapacious man, he was mistrusted by all who had dealings with him but tenaciously hung on to power and outlived all his enemies. Magrath had trained as a Franciscan friar and was first appointed Catholic bishop of Down and Connor in 1565. A couple of years later he decided to switch allegiance to the new reformed Anglican Church and the following year Queen Elizabeth appointed him Archbishop of Cashel. In all, he held four bishoprics simultaneously, all of which he neglected and failed to make any provision for services. He even managed for nine years to be both a Catholic bishop and an Anglican archbishop, until finally an exasperated Pope accused him of heresy and deprived him of the see of Down and Connor. He was later forced to resign Waterford and Lismore because of his neglect of his duties but somehow managed to hang on to Cashel and then to acquire Killala. Magrath was adept at intrigue, collaborating with the government and informing upon rebels, then promptly switching sides and intriguing with his erstwhile opponents.

MULLINAHONE

Charles Kickham (1828–1882), the novelist and patriot, is buried in Mullinahone. The epitaph inscribed on the Celtic cross over his grave was written by the Fenian, John O'Leary (see Glasnevin).

> *Journalist, novelist, poet*
> *But before all patriot*
> *Traitor to crime, to vice and fraud*
> *but true to Ireland and to God.*

In 1865 Kickham was arrested and sentenced to fourteen years penal servitude but was released after only four years when his health collapsed. He had never enjoyed good health in any case as he had injured both his sight and his hearing in a gun accident in childhood. After his release he devoted the rest of his life to writing. His best regarded novel was *Knocknagow*, written about 1879.

SHANRAHAN

Kickham's novel, *Knocknagow*, was based on the story of **Rev Nicholas Sheehy** (1728–1766), a priest who had been hanged in Clonmel, the "town with a cloud over it". Father Sheehy had been an outspoken critic of the established church and its demands of heavy tithes from the impoverished Catholic tenant farmers. Inevitably this led to allegations that he was involved with the local Whiteboys. He was accused of the murder of an informer, John Bridge, but, believing that he had no chance of a fair trial in Clonmel, went on the run. Several months later, he gave himself up on condition that the trial would take place in Dublin. At this trial he was acquitted of involvement with the Whiteboys but was immediately re-arrested and sent to Clonmel for trial as an accessory to murder. Despite the crown's weak case, he was condemned to death on perjured evidence. Father Sheehy was hanged, drawn and quartered and his head impaled at the entrance to the jail house. He was buried in the grounds of the now ruined church at Shanrahan where his grave soon became a place of pilgrimage. There is a memorial plaque at the gate.

TUBRID

The poet and historian, **Geoffrey Keating** or **Seathrún Céitin** (c.1570 – c.1640), is buried in the grounds of another ruined church nearby at Tubrid. There is a memorial tablet at the gate and another inside the remains of the church over his burial-place. Keating was educated at a local bardic school and at the Irish College of Bordeaux where he studied theology. He returned as a priest to Tipperary about 1610 and then commenced writing his *History of Ireland* or *Foras Feasa ar Eirinn*, travelling all over the country to examine manuscripts and papers in the possession of the old Gaelic and Norman families. (He was himself of Norman stock.) There is a further monument to Keating at his birthplace at Burgess.

KNOCKLOFTY

The soldier, **John Hely-Hutchinson** (1757–1832), the second Earl of Donoughmore, was in command of 1,500 men, mostly fencibles and disaffected Irish militiamen, at Castlebar when the French landed at Killala Bay in the rebellion of August 1798. Many of his troops fled when the French approached, in the rout that came to be known as "the races of Castlebar". Hely-Hutchinson later fought against Napoleonic forces in the Peninsular wars, in Italy and in Egypt.

One of the inner circle of friends of "Prinny", King George

IV, Lord Hutchinson was sent on an unsuccessful mission to offer the king's wayward and estranged wife, Queen Caroline, a generous settlement if she would agree to stay out of England and not make an appearance at his Coronation. She did not agree to his terms. In the *Dictionary of National Biography*, his Lordship is described as being very ugly, "with harsh features jaundiced by disease, extreme short-sightedness, a stooping body, a slouching gait and an utter neglect of his dress." He died at Knocklofty in Tipperary and is buried in the old Church of Ireland there as are several other Earls of Donoughmore.

THURLES

The close of the summer in rural and not so rural areas is marked by the sudden appearance of county flags and banners flying at every lamp-post, telegraph pole and filling station as the provincial champions of hurling and football enter the fray to "bring home the cup" from the All Ireland Finals held in Croke Park in Dublin. The eponymous Croke, **Thomas William Croke** (1823–1902), was Archbishop of Cashel and Emly and the first patron of the GAA.

A very influential figure in the politics of his day, Croke was a supporter of Davitt's Land League and of Parnell's advocacy of Home Rule for Ireland. He was one of the founder members of the Gaelic Athletics Association in 1884. At the time, there were no organised games in rural Ireland, a consequence of recurring famine, mass emigration and little leisure time for those who remained. The GAA set out to revive and regulate the rules of the old games of Gaelic football, hurling and handball which rapidly enjoyed a huge surge of popularity. Archbishop Croke is buried in the mortuary chapel of Thurles Cathedral in a vault on the left hand side of the high altar.

Dan Breen (1894–1969), the Republican politician and IRA leader during the War of Independence, is buried in Donohill a few miles outside Tipperary town.

On 21 January 1919, the day that the Dáil first met in the Mansion House in Dublin, he led an ambush on a party of policemen escorting explosives to a quarry in Soloheadbeg, the incident that marked the beginning of the War of Independence and the first assault on British forces since the Rising in Easter 1916. Breen went on the run with a price on his head of £1,000.

With Sean Treacy, he shot his way out of a house in Drumcondra in Dublin through a cordon of soldiers and escaped but was badly wounded. After the war he was elected TD for Tipperary in 1923 but did not take his seat until 1927, the first anti-Treaty member to do so. His autobiographical account of his life as a guerrilla fighter, *My Fight For Irish Freedom*, was published in 1924.

WATERFORD

Edmund Ignatius Rice (1762–1844), the founder of the Christian Brothers, was buried until recently in a mausoleum in Mount Sion in Waterford but now, in an excess of zeal, his remains lie in a coffin behind a glass wall in the memorial chapel. He was beatified by Pope John Paul II in October 1996. Rice was a wealthy businessman who, heartbroken by the premature death of his wife in childbirth, gave up his business, locked up his home and devoted himself to charitable works. He founded the first of many schools for poor boys in Waterford in 1803, their teachers a community of lay brothers. By the time he retired there were more than twenty similar schools in Britain and Ireland. Since then the Christian Brothers have founded schools all over the world and provided an education to generations of Catholic youths, though not always untouched by controversy.

> *"I am now what you will become.*
> *I once was what you are now."*

So says the epitaph on a macabre tomb in Christchurch Cathedral in Waterford, dedicated to an earlier Rice. This is the burial place of the pious merchant and several times mayor of the city, **James Rice**. Sometime in the late 1400s, he had a memorial chapel built on to the side of the cathedral to house his tomb. It depicts a life-size stone skeleton, with the shroud pulled back to expose the worms crawling around the ribs and limbs. A frog is perched atop his belly. This blatant reminder of man's mortality was commissioned to Rice's own specifications to serve as a reminder to posterity that neither riches nor high position prevail. Death is the great leveller.

NEWTOWN, NEAR KILMACTHOMAS

"The most celebrated of all the bards," **Donnchad Ruadh McNamara** (1715–1810) is buried in Newtown churchyard. The gravestone is on the wall on your left as your enter – it was erected on the centenary of his death with subscriptions from the Waterford and SE Archaeological society. There are lavish inscriptions in both Latin and Irish attesting to his pre-eminence as a Gaelic poet.

In the mid 1700s Donnchadh Ruadh had spent some years in Newfoundland, one of many Waterford men who went to work on the rich fishing grounds there and escape the economic hardship of home. Throughout the sixteenth, seventeenth and eighteenth centuries, the British fleet used to call into Waterford to take on provisions and recruit men who would be indentured to spend two summers and a winter in Newfoundland, fishing first for herring to be used as bait, then spending the summer catching and curing the salt cod. St John's and the area around Avalon had an Irish population that in 1750 outnumbered the British, the French and the Portuguese. McNamara's poems describe the hard-working, hard-playing lifestyle of the Irish population, the hurling matches and fights between the Leinster and Munstermen, the drinking and carousing, the agony and misery of the weeks pursuing the fish, and the pain and cold that had to be endured while they plunged the cod into the pickling brine. For a while McNamara is believed to have run a school in the colony as the indentured men began to settle after their contracts were up and a merchant class began to emerge but, some time in the 1750s, he became disillusioned with life in Newfoundland and returned to live in Ireland and travel in Europe. His friend, **Tadhg O'Suilleabháin** (1715–1795), also a Gaelic bard, is buried in the churchyard of Ballylaneen.

DUNGARVAN

In St Mary's Church of Ireland cemetery, a grave simply inscribed **"Moresby Mass Grave 1895"** commemorates the victims of a shipwreck on Christmas Eve of that year.

The *Moresby* had sailed out of Cardiff on 21 December with a crew of twenty-three, including Captain Francis Coomber, accompanied by his wife and infant daughter. The ship almost immediately got into difficulties and set anchor off Dungarvan the following day. A lifeboat went out to them but was sent away as no one wished to leave. The weather continued to deteriorate and early on the morning of Christmas Eve, the ship broke anchor. The crew sent up distress flares. The ship began to break asunder. Men were vainly trying to cling to the wreckage as they were pitched into the sea and still no help came from the shore. It was not until mid-day that the Ballinacourty lifeboat at last arrived and rescued four men – one of them Henry Blount who, after spending Christmas Day in hospital, had the unenviable task of identifying the bodies of his colleagues as they were washed ashore, the baby daughter of Captain Coomber being the last body to be recovered. Most of the dead were buried together in St Mary's in a mass grave though six other victims were buried separately. The enquiry into the disaster investigated the delay in the rescue attempt and found the Honorary Secretary of the Lifeboat Association, the chief boatman of the coastguards and the coxswain of the lifeboat "had not acted appropriately." The whole sorry affair seemed to have been surrounded by controversy. Wrangling dragged on for months about whose responsibility it was to salvage the wreck which was a danger and obstacle to other ships entering and leaving the harbour. Eventually a plaque to commemorate the lifeboatmen for their valour was erected between the park and the churchyard.

LISMORE

In Lismore Cathedral there is an unusual grave stone dated 1557 which has carvings of a cock and a cooking pot. It is one of only a few examples of this design in the country. Apparently it is based on a story which is found in old Greek manuscripts and crops up in some early Irish manuscripts. After betraying Christ, Judas Iscariot returned home and asked his wife to give him a rope to hang himself for he knew that Christ would rise again. His wife declared that that was as likely as the cock in her pot coming back to life, whereupon the cock duly flapped its wings, flew onto the side of the pot and crowed thrice. A gravestone slab of similar date and design can be seen on the aisle of Kilkenny cathedral.

ULSTER

ANTRIM

BELFAST

Both **Henry Joy McCracken** (1767–1798) and his sister **Mary Ann** (1770–1866) are buried in the tranquil walled graveyard called the New Burying Ground, in Clifton Street. McCracken was one of the founders of the first group of United Irishmen in Belfast and was the principal leader of the rebellion in Antrim in 1798. Captured after a period on the run in the Slemish mountains, he was tried and hanged for treason in Belfast. He was first buried in St George's but his remains were re-interred in his sister's grave in 1909. Mary Ann's headstone says that she was "the beloved sister of Henry Joy McCracken, born 8 July 1770, wept by her brother's scaffold, 17 July 1798, died 26 July 1866. Dileas go h-éag (faithful unto death)". Mary-Ann described the scene at the Cornmarket before his execution:

About 5 p.m. he was ordered to the place of execution, the old market-house, the ground of which had been given to the town by his great great grandfather. I took his arm, and we walked together to the place of execution, where I was told it was the General's orders I should leave him, which I peremptorily refused. Harry begged I should go. Clasping my hands around him (I did not weep till then), I said I could bear any thing but leaving him. Three times he kissed me, and entreated I would go . . . and fearing any further refusal would

disturb the last moments of my dearest brother, I suffered
myself to be led away . . .

In the aftermath of the failed rebellion, Mary Ann gave much charitable help to the relatives of all those who were executed. She was responsible for erecting the tombstones over many of their graves, including that of Thomas Russell (see Downpatrick). In her later years she was active in campaigns to abolish child labour and provide education for destitute children.

Also in the New Burying Ground is the monument to their grandfather, **Henry Joy**. The Joy family were proprietors of the *Belfast Newsletter*, first published in 1737 and the oldest surviving newspaper in the British Isles.

William Drennan (1754–1820), a medical doctor, son of a Presbyterian minister and the author of the original prospectus of the United Irishmen, is also buried here. Although a founder member of the movement, he was acquitted of sedition and did not get involved in the eventual rebellion in 1798. He was the first person to call Ireland "the Emerald Isle" in a poem published in 1795. The epitaph reads :

> *Pure, just, benign: thus filial love would trace*
> *The Virtues hallowing this narrow space,*
> *The Emerald Isle may grant a wider claim,*
> *And link the patriot with his Country's name.*

The **Reverend William Steel Dickson** (1744–1824), another United Irishman, is buried in the paupers' ground of the graveyard. He was Adjutant-General of Down but was imprisoned just before the crucial Battle of Ballynahinch. He spent a year in a prison hulk and three years in Fort George together with Thomas Russell (see Downpatrick, County Down). He died in obscurity and poverty. The headstone on his grave was erected earlier this century by the Belfast folklorist and antiquarian FJ Biggar who was also responsible for re-interring Henry Joy McCracken with his sister. The epitaph is "Do cum onora na h-Éireann."

There is an enigmatic, but brutally frank, gravestone on the north wall in this cemetery which reads "Young! moulders here! 1829". This is the grave of **John Young** (1781–1829), Professor of Moral Philosophy at the Belfast Academical Institution, the forerunner of Queen's University. Some time before his death, when accepting the gift of a silk gown from his students, he had said "I have endeavoured to train you so that you may be imbued with an ardent and unalterable love of truth, and it is my dearest wish that this could be written, with justice, on my tomb." Heaven knows why he ended up with such a strange inscription and its oddly placed exclamation mark.

Sir Edward Carson (1854–1935) was the Dublin lawyer who led the opposition to Home Rule when it was beginning to look inevitable in the years before the outbreak of the First World War. He established the formidable Ulster Volunteer Force with over 90,000 members, and imported vast armaments of rifles and ammunition which no doubt would have fuelled a civil war had Home Rule for Ireland gone ahead. He was the leader of the Ulster Unionist party between 1911 and 1922. Carson is also to be remembered as the barrister who devastatingly cross-examined Oscar Wilde at his libel trial. He was buried in the south aisle of St Anne's Cathedral after a state funeral. It is the only tomb in the cathedral.

James Craig, Lord Craigavon (1871–1940), led the resistance to Home Rule with Carson, instigating mass demonstrations across the province and setting up Ulster Day in September 1912 when almost half a million Ulstermen signed the Covenant of Resistance. After the general election of 1921, when the Unionists won a huge majority, he became the first Prime Minister of Northern Ireland and remained premier from then until his death. The *Irish Times* wrote of him:

"For the better part of a generation, he was the symbol of

Northern Irish Unionism. His personality was the sheet anchor of a tradition that went back to the Apprentice Boys of Derry, and the day may come when Ireland will remember him with feelings of pride." He was buried in the grounds of Stormont Castle, on the east side of Parliament Buildings.

KNOCKNACARRY

There is a curious tombstone in the Catholic churchyard at Knocknacarry, two miles south of Cushendun. It has a crude drawing of a sailing ship moored to two anchors with lengths of cable and a goat standing to one side. The inexpertly carved inscription reads:

> *Charles McAlasters Burr*
> *Ing Place*
> *here lies the*
> *boddy of John*
> *His son died 11*
> *March 1803*
> *aged 18 years*
> *"Your ship*
> *Love is mor*
> *ed head and*
> *starn for a fuldiew*

The story goes that **John McAlaster** (d.1803) was courting a girl from Cushendun, went to sea, but was killed when he fell from the mast of the schooner on the very eve his ship was returning to Cushendun. When she heard the news that her lover had been killed, the girl disappeared and was found dead the following morning lying on the tombstone having apparently spent the night carving these words on to the stone. The "fuldiew" may be "the full due", a naval expression meaning all the leave and entitlements accrued during a voyage, perhaps a reference to the fact that John's life was over and he was now called to account. John's father, Charles McAlaster, incidentally had sailed with Nelson when he was a boy.

If you are in the area, you might like to cross the road where, opposite the church, is the Gloonan stone, the site of one of the many St Patrick's wells in this area. The stone, according to tradition, has an imprint of the saint's knee. (The word Gloonan comes from the Irish word for knee.) At the time of my visit the well and surrounding area was in lamentable condition.

GLENAAN, NEAR CUSHENDALL

There are many ancient sites associated with the Fianna, the legendary heroes of the Ulster Cycle, here in the splendid glens of Antrim. If you follow the road out of Cushendall towards Cushendun you will see the signposts for the tomb of **Ossian**. At the sign, leave your car and walk up the hill for about half a mile where you will eventually find a field in which there are the remains of a court tomb. Ossian, or Oisín as he is also known, was the warrior-poet son of Finn Mac Cool. He fell in love with Niamh Cinn Oir, Niamh of the Golden Hair, and returned with her to her home in Tír na nÓg (Land of Eternal Youth). After a while, he longed to come back to see his old friends again and was allowed with the proviso that he must not get down from his horse. When he arrived back in Ireland, he saw a number of men struggling to raise a boulder. Appalled at their lack of strength, he jumped down from the saddle. But as soon as his feet touched the earth, he was transformed into an old, old man. He had been gone, not one or two years, but hundreds! Be that as it may, tradition has it that he is buried here in Ossian's Tomb, though the tomb is probably at least four or five thousand years old. Among the yellow whin bushes, you can see the remains of a cairn, originally oval in shape, with a pair of portal stones leading into a burial gallery. It has not been excavated.

The surprise for anyone who gets this far is to see in the same field another cairn in the shape of a beehive cell with the inscription "My Chosen Ground". This is the final burial place of the Ulster poet, **John Hewitt**, (1907–1987), presiding over a magnificent view of the glens.

LAYDE

Also near Cushendall, just outside the village in a lovely valley beside a fast-flowing stream, is a little gem of a ruined mediaeval church. It was probably in use for about a thousand years, being valued at twenty shillings in 1306, but finally fell into disuse in the late eighteenth century. The last clergymen here were the **Reverend John McArthur** (d.1749), and his son, **Rev Dennis McArthur** (d.1796), both of whom are interred under the floor of the church. Buried here in Layde are many Macauleys and MacDonnells, influential settler families in the plantation of Ulster (there are Mac Donnell castles all around Antrim). Supporters of Charles I, the king beheaded by Cromwell in 1649, their tombs commemorate the many soldiers of the families and their deaths in battles and campaigns in Scotland and Ireland. There is also a high Celtic cross decorated with Biblical scenes of healing, which commemorates **Dr James McDonnell**, born in 1762, who founded the Belfast Dispensary near Smithfield. It was the first in Belfast to provide free medicine and free medical care to the poor.

It is curious to see how burials in this place have altered the shape of the land around the church which is all bumps and hummocks. The burials inside the church in the Macauley vaults have raised the level inside by at least a metre so that the windows are now almost at present-day ground level. It must always have been a striking place, this little green valley with its noisy river, and the bright red stone of the church which would once have been topped by a yellow thatch. Outside the gateway, there are two slabs of stone, known as "corpstanes" which were used to rest the coffins on before carrying them through to the graveyard.

MALLUSK

James (Jenny) Hope (1764–1847) is buried at Mallusk,

near Templepatrick. He was a Presbyterian United Irishman who took part in the disastrous and bloody battle of Ballynahinch with General Munro and his army of pikemen. He escaped to Dublin but returned north to work as a linen weaver after the amnesty of 1806. The epitaph on the marble tablet erected by Mary Ann McCracken describes him as "one of nature's noblest works, an honest man. Steadfast in faith and always hopeful in the Divine protection. In the best years of his country's history a soldier in her cause, and in the worst of times still faithful to her; ever true to himself and to those who trusted in him, he remained to the last unchanged and unchangeable in his fidelity."

In his memoirs he wrote of both the 1798 and 1803 rebellions and described how the United Irishmen sought to bring the republican principles of liberty, equality and fraternity to Ireland. He paid tribute to Neilson, Russell, McCracken and all those who died or were executed during the rebellion. He remained a staunch Presbyterian and commendably wrote on the question of religion: "I wish to let my neighbours' creed alone; I think it quite enough to mind my own."

LARNE

One of several Irishmen who left precise instructions for their burial was **James Chaine** (d.1885), an eccentric entrepreneur who sat as MP for County Antrim between 1874–1885. At his own request he is interred on a hillside overlooking Larne harbour (which he had been influential in developing) in an upright position, facing the sea and wearing his full yachting attire. The grave is accessible from the town park.

DONEGORE

The antiquary, **Sir Samuel Ferguson** (1810–1886), is buried in an old churchyard in Donegore, east of Antrim. He was a poet, folklorist and the first person to be appointed Deputy Keeper of the Records of Ireland. He made many translations of old Irish songs, legends and poems and wrote extensively on the antiquities of Ireland, including a master work on the ogham inscriptions, the ancient alphabet and system of writing used by the Irish which is to be found on many of the oldest Irish grave stones. Ferguson was also a prolific poet. There is a monument to him and to Lady Ferguson in St Patrick's Cathedral, Dublin which was unveiled in 1907, "two gifted authors in the field of Celtic literature whose memories are blessed".

His native Antrim is also the final resting-place of the poet **Louis MacNeice** (1907–1963) even though he had a very strained relationship with the country. Born in Belfast and brought up in the vicarage at Carrickfergus where his father was rector, he left Ireland for Oxford where he was a contemporary of Auden and Spender. A liberal thoughtful man, he wrote "I cannot be/Anyone else than what this land engendered me" but needed to strike out, to leave behind the complications of belonging to the Protestant upper class in Ireland. His ashes are interred in his mother's grave in Carrowdore churchyard.

Fans of unusual monuments or old gravestone inscriptions will find plenty in County Antrim. At Castle Upton, on the outskirts of Belfast, the Templeton mausoleum of the Rt. Hon. Arthur Upton is a remarkable structure built by the architect Robert Adam in 1789. Around this time tomb-building in both Britain and Ireland was very much influenced by the archaeology and architecture of ancient Greece and Rome. A mausoleum was the perfect vehicle for an architect to express classical forms without any need to concern himself with the provision of heating or light. Adam designed a number of mausoleums, of which this is the best remaining example in Ireland. It is now in the hands of the National Trust.

A similar desire to make a strong architectural statement is to be found in the Kilbride graveyard where the Stephenson family, inspired by army service in India, erected a scaled-down replica of the Taj Mahal, complete with dome, in 1837.

In All Saints Church of Ireland in Ballymoney, among the many memorials to the McCartney family is one dedicated to **Ellen McCartney**, who died 15 March 1847. Its enigmatic inscription tells us that "She was summoned in all fulness (but without suffering) to another and better world by the awful yet merciful decree of a divine providence owing to the accidental explosion of a quantity of gunpowder."

Most grave inscriptions throughout Ireland are written in English or Latin; occasionally one comes across stones inscribed in Irish though not as often as one would expect given that it was the majority language in the country for hundreds of years. In Derrykeighan graveyard, there is an epitaph in a language that once would have been common in Ulster: Scots. It reads "Hier lyith the corpis of ane fathful sistir in the Lord calid **Margrat Boyd**."

And finally, in the old graveyard at Ramoan, near Ballycastle, there are two tall eighteenth century tombstones "cutt by Alexr. McDonnell" which are worth hunting for. One commemorates **Archibald McCambridge** who died in 1784 and the other **Francis Boyd** (1788). Both stones have an inset panel carved with a skull and crossbones. The inscription on McCambridge's tombstone says *Memento Mori* but the sculptor has translated this on Boyd's tombstone as "Remember to die" – as if we had any choice in the matter!

ARMAGH

Brian Boru (c.941– 1014), King of Ireland, was killed in his tent by defeated Norsemen after the Battle of Clontarf on Good Friday, 23 April 1014. This decisive battle, popularly believed to have been the last great struggle between the native Irish and the Vikings, was really an internal revolt against Brian's rule by the Leinstermen. Ulster and most of Connacht did not take part at all. On Brian Boru's side were Munster and South Connacht ranged against Leinster and the Vikings with additional support from Vikings from the Isle of Man. There were huge losses on both sides and although Brian's side was victorious, he, his son Murrough and many of the leading Munstermen were all slain. Their bodies were taken to Armagh, the religious and spiritual centre of Ireland, to lie in state for twelve days before being buried with great ceremony. Of course nothing now remains of that church – the present Church of Ireland cathedral mostly dates from the nineteenth century built on thirteenth century ruins – and the precise location of the king's tomb has long been forgotten. However there is a modern plaque on the outside wall of the north transept which says that that "near this spot on the north side of the great church was laid the body of Brian Boroimhe slain at Clontarf AD MXIV".

No such doubt surrounds the location of the burial of **Harriet D'Arcy**, the wife of a former Archbishop of Armagh as the memorial plaque on the wall inside the cathedral reveals. The lady in question died at sea while accompanying her husband on a retirement cruise. Her memorial gives the precise latitude and longitude of her burial in the middle of the Atlantic ocean.

Within the cathedral the memorials are mostly to the deans and other ecclesiastical figures. In the north aisle there is an imposing marble tomb with a full-size figure of **Peter Drelincourt** who was Dean from 1691–1722, erected according to the inscription by *"one who shar'd his bed and mind"*. As a further memorial to her husband, Mrs Drelincourt endowed the Drelincourt School, which is still a junior school.

ARMAGH, ST MARK'S CHURCH

A railway disaster occurred in June 1889 which then had the dubious distinction of being the worst railway accident up to that time with the greatest loss of life. Eighty people died, including many young children who were on a Sunday school outing from the Methodist church. The packed train had left Armagh bound for an excursion to Warrenpoint. The engine stalled at the top of a steep gradient and ten carriages slid backwards into an oncoming train. Five members of the **Cleeland family**, James and Margaret and their three children, all died in the crash. They and many more victims of the disaster were buried in the churchyard of St Mark's, the parish church of Armagh. A book, *The Fateful Day*, by Damian Woods, includes a map of the graveyard showing the location of the graves. There is also a memorial plaque in the Methodist church giving the names of all the victims. The investigation which followed the Armagh disaster led to new safety legislation for all the British railway networks and to the introduction of vacuum brakes on all trains.

CREGGAN

For such a small townland, the multi-denominational

graveyard at Creggan has more than its fair share of fascinating graves of poets, rapparees, priests, powerful landlords and chieftains, not to mention an enigmatic building which has been the object of recent study by academics and Armagh observatory.

The family vault of the **O'Neills of the Fews** of Glassdrummond Castle contains the bodies of all the O'Neills who died 1480–1820. It is quite a shock to enter and see the piles of bones and skulls heaped up on the ground – there are at least seventy intact skulls, many of them with impressive sets of teeth, lying on top of the bleached piles of femurs, hip bones and tibia. The vault had been closed up and forgotten about for well over a century until, during maintenance work in 1971, a tractor wheel sank into the ground above it and its existence was rediscovered. The vault may be visited on application to the rector or to the Creggan Historical Society. Set into the wall on the way down the newly restored steps is part of an old headstone with a carving of the Red Hand of Ulster. It marked the grave of **Art Óg Ó Neill** who died in 1769 at the age of twenty-six, the last son of the last of the Ó Neill chieftains. The poet Art MacCooey wrote a lament to him, regarding his early death a national disaster.

The said **Art MacCooey** (1739–1773) is also buried in Creggan. A headstone designed by John Behan was erected in 1973, the bicentenary of his death, on his reputed burial place. About twenty-five of his poems have survived, mainly satires on the vanity of the new Irish middle classes, on priests and inhospitable women, laments for Ireland and the last of its chiefs. The last two lines of his poem "Urchill an Chreagáin" ("The Noble Churchyard of Creggan") are inscribed on the stone:

"A gaeil chumhra an Chreagáin a leafgar mé in gcré faoi fód."
(In the fragrant clay of Creggan let my weary heart have rest.)

MacCooey was a colourful character, a well-educated spendthrift who squandered his inheritance and spent most of his life working as a labourer. Forbidden to marry his cousin, Mary Lamb, he found a sympathetic priest who married him in Creggan but was promptly excommunicated by the parish priest and forced to leave the area. About a year later the order was revoked by the Vicar General of Armagh and he returned to live in the area. The priest who excommunicated him, **Fr Terence Quinn**, (d.1775 aged sixty) is also buried here – the original flat stone is almost illegible now but there is a modern transcription.

Near the wall of the church is the grave of **Séamus Mór MacMurphy** (?1720–1760) of Carnally. He is described as "file agus Tóraidhe" (poet and Tory) on the headstone. It is ironic that the word Tory has now become synonymous with the British Conservative party for the word was originally used to describe Roman Catholic outlaws. MacMurphy's life has all the elements of a melodrama. He was a supporter of Charles Stuart, the Young Pretender Bonnie Prince Charlie, who, it was hoped, was going to come to Ireland to seize the throne. While on the run, MacMurphy was betrayed by a woman whom he had slighted. (Like many other eighteenth century Gaelic poets, MacMurphy was both promiscuous and a heavy drinker.) Molly MacDacker, the daughter of a squint-eyed shebeen owner, plied his fellow-poet Peadar Ó Doirnín with drink and got him to write a poem "The Heretic Headcutter" attacking John Johnston, the tory-hunter. She then took the poem to Johnston but attributed it to MacMurphy and offered to help in his capture for the not inconsiderable sum of fifty pounds.

MacMurphy's captor, **John Johnston** of the Fews, was the chief constable of the barony of the Fews in 1710 and is buried only a few yards away in the burial plot of the Johnstons in a walled off area. The Johnstons were the most powerful family in the Fews in the eighteenth century and were reviled by the contemporary poets who frequently lambasted them in their verse. John Johnston was so particularly despised and so successful and ruthless a bandit-hunter that his exploits gave rise to the refrain:

Jesus of Nazareth, King of the Jews
save us from Johnston, King of the Fews.

The hapless MacMurphy was duly delivered up to Johnston and hanged, having been found guilty of stealing a horse though the lampoon was the real crime. Mollie subsequently drowned herself and is buried in an unmarked grave in Narrow Water in the part of the graveyard set aside for suicides and unbaptised babies.

A small oratory-like structure in Creggan churchyard was for many years the vault of another local landord family, the Eastwoods, though recent research appears to demonstrate that it is much older. Local tradition held that it had been a watch house to deter grave robbers and while that may indeed have been the case, it certainly wasn't built for that purpose. It is now suggested that it was the site of an early Christian church founded in the fifth century. It has a stone barrel-vaulted roof and one small narrow window with splayed sill. Its orientation is west to east and there is a small recess in one wall which might suggest a repository for chalice and patten. It is possible to discern the marks left behind on the walls by the original, and now calcified, osier and wattle framework. In the first recorded instance of astronomy being employed on a monastic site, Armagh observatory have shown that the sun rises on the morning of February 11th through the narrow east window. This is the date of the feast-day of Jarlath, a local saint, a contemporary of St Patrick, who became the third bishop of Armagh. Could this have been his burial place, his shrine?

There are several interesting plaques in the graveyard, including one commemorating a priest who was ordained by Saint Oliver Plunkett (see Drogheda), and one to **Patrick Mac aLiondain** (died 1733), another Gaelic poet and harper who was patron of the other poets of the Fews and the composer of a "Lament to Eoghan Rua Ó Neill" (see Cavan). A number of graves have United Irishmen associations. A helpful booklet on Creggan churchyard has been produced by the local historical society. It must surely rank as one of the most fascinating burial grounds in the country.

Urnai

Peadar Ó Doirnín (1704–1769 or 1682–1769 – sources differ), the Gaelic poet and schoolmaster at Forkhill, is buried at Urnaí, three miles north of Dundalk, more or less on the border of counties Armagh and Louth. The grave, marked by a strangely sculptured upright stone, is at the rear of the graveyard, near the hedge. Ó Doirnín wrote mainly political verse and pastoral romantic love poems though, in the best tradition of Gaelic poetry, these can have unexpectedly bawdy twists. In one, he pleads to his lover to come away with him. He offers her the prospect of swimming in smooth cold lakes and listening to him play the harp with swift fingers. The final verse is the lover's bawdy retort "I wouldn't accept noble lands, cattle, sheep, piles of pearls in palaces from you if you had no instrument to make a child at bed-time".

Ó Doirnín's school of poetry was banned by Johnston of the Fews and he was outlawed as a "person ill-disposed to the king, a favourite of the Pretender . . . who stirs up people to rebel by his treasonable composition." As mentioned above, he was a contemporary and friend of the poet and executed outlaw Séamus Mór MacMurphy and played an unwitting part in his capture by composing the lampoon to John Johnston.

An unusual feature of this old graveyard is the number of gravestones inscribed in Irish, including several in the immediate vicinity of Ó Doirnín. One is over the grave of a United Irishman, Tomás Ó Cappaid, killed in the 1798 rebellion.

The graveyard itself is rather difficult to find. On the T23 road between Armagh and Dundalk, it is signposted $1^{1/2}$ miles.

Keep to the right where there is a sign saying "lay-by", then go through a gate marked by two stone pillars and across a field.

RELICARN, NR SCARVA

Yet another "tory" outlaw, **Redmond O'Hanlon**, (died 1681) was the descendant of a family who had been dispossessed of their estates by Cromwell. He led a gang of outlaws who exacted tributes in Tyrone and Armagh and for years managed to evade capture. Finally, with a price of £200 on his head, he was murdered for the reward by his foster-brother. The head in question was ignominiously spiked at Downpatrick jail. (These men may have known their enemies but were on less sure grounds with their friends.) O'Hanlon was buried in the old graveyard at Relicarn, between Tandragee and Scarva one mile from Scarva. The grave is not marked and may now lie under the road which has been realigned.

CAVAN

Two graves in Cavan are associated with the 1641 Ulster rebellion and its aftermath.

The great reforming bishop, **William Bedell** (1571–1642), is buried in the graveyard of Kilmore Church of Ireland Cathedral three miles outside Cavan town. Bedell, an Englishman, was the first to translate the Old Testament into Irish in the belief that the use of the scriptures in the vernacular was the only effective means of bringing the Reformation to Ireland. This was very controversial at the time since Parliament, far from wanting to endorse the use of Irish, was more disposed to suppress it. As provost of Trinity College he had ruled that all students who were born in Ireland should study Irish. He opposed the penal law enactments and the exaction of huge tithes from Catholics. Bedell finished his translation in 1640 just a year before the outbreak of war in Ulster. He was imprisoned briefly in Cloughoughter castle in 1642, contracted a fever from refugees from the war and died.

As the funeral was making its way to the churchyard, O'Reilly, the local chieftain, approached leading a party of musketeers and a drummer. The mourners were afraid that the rebels were about to disrupt the burial. Instead, as the bishop's son wrote:

it prov'd no such thing. For O Relly and those with him applied themselves in most courteous and condoling

*language, speaking respectfully and honourably of the dead
and confortably to the living; and so, commanding their drum
to beat, as the manner is when a souldier is buried, and
placing the musqueteers before the corps, they thus
conveighed the bishop to his grave . . . and when all was
done, he commanded the musqueteers to give a volley of shot,
and so the company departed.*

Bedell's Old Testament was eventually printed in London
in 1685, financed by the Irish scientist and philosopher Robert
Boyle. The first fifty copies were presented to Narcissus
Marsh, then provost of Trinity College in Dublin, for the use
of divinity students.

At the rear of Bedell's tomb, there is now a small private
graveyard where a number of more recent Bishops of Kilmore
are buried.

Owen Roe O'Neill, (c.1590–1649), was one of the military
commanders throughout the lengthy war which followed the
Ulster rebellion of 1641. A nephew of Hugh O'Neill, one of the
earls whose flight in 1607 precipitated the plantation of Ulster,
Owen Roe O'Neill had fought in the Spanish army for thirty
years but came to Ireland in June 1642 when he was made
commander of the Irish forces. In 1646 he defeated General
Monro at the Battle of Benburb, the only major battle of the
campaign that the Irish won. O'Neill was on his way south –
Cromwell had by then arrived in Ireland and had launched his
devastating crusade with the capture of Drogheda and Wexford
– but was in increasingly poor health. He died in November in
Cavan and was buried in the chancel of the Franciscan friary.
There were rumours that he had been poisoned but there is no
concrete evidence to support this. All but the tower of the friary
has now been demolished but there is a memorial plaque on the
tower in commemoration of *"The Victor of Benburb"*.

Another plaque records that **Myles "The Slasher" O'Reilly**
is also buried in these grounds. He was slain in the historic
defence of Finea Bridge against the crown forces in 1644.

DERRY

Derry is the Maiden City of Ireland, so-called because its still impressive walls remained unbreached by the Jacobite forces during the 1689 siege of the city. **Colonel Henry Baker** (d.1689), governor of the city at the time of the siege and **Michael Browning** (d.1689), captain of the *Mountjoy*, the ship that broke the boom across the river Foyle, are both buried in St Columb's Cathedral.

The plaque on the north aisle tells us that Baker died on 30 June 1689 on the 74th day of the siege "worn out by hardship and disease". Despite a violent fever he had insisted upon staying out on the walls all night to encourage his men in anticipation of enemy attack.

The siege officially began on 17 April when King James's forces advanced upon the city and were fired upon by the defenders of the walled city crying "No surrender". Conditions within the walls rapidly became atrocious. There was dire overcrowding as local Protestants had been gathering in the city for months beforehand. It is thought that as few as eighty people died in the fighting but that thousands died from hunger and disease. As the food shortages worsened, lists were posted setting the price of a dog's head (two shillings and six pence), a cat (one shilling and sixpence) a rat (one shilling) or a piece of horse flesh (one shilling and eight pence per pound weight). The besieged citizens were even reduced to eating an unpalatable mixture of tallow and starch which not only filled the belly but "was an infallible cure for the looseness" according to a contemporary account. By 28 July, the Reverend George Walker, joint governor with Baker, recorded that of 7,500 men at the start of the siege only 4,300 were still alive and of them one quarter were unfit for fighting. With no place to bury them, thousands of the dead were just dumped in cellars or buried in backyards – even in modern times human skeletons dating from these times are found in the city.

King James's forces were badly equipped, so apart from hurling mortar bombs at the city, their tactics were simply to force the city to submit by starving them and to prevent relief ships from coming up the river. To do so they constructed a boom across the river Foyle. By the end of July when Governor Walker reckoned the besieged city had no more than two days of life, three relief ships arrived and attacked the boom. **Michael Browning**, a native of Derry, was captain of the *Mountjoy*, the ship that broke through first. As the memorial in the cathedral notes, "he was killed at the boom in the hour of victory while encouraging his men in the face of terrible danger on the 28th July 1689." Three days later on 1 August, King James and his army conceded defeat and began to retreat from the city. The siege had lasted 105 days.

But despite the jubilation and celebrations within the walls, the aftermath of the siege was to bring more disappointments. In spite of numerous commissions and recommendations, King William and his Parliament paid neither the monies due in wages to the defenders nor the grants to rebuild their ruined city. One of the Derrymen who tried to press the case for compensation was **Colonel John Mitchelburne** (d.1721) who had been appointed governor of the city after Colonel Baker's death. Indeed, when he went to London in 1709, he was not only fobbed off but ended up in a debtors' prison. Mitchelburne, who had lost both his wife and all his children to starvation and fever, was the author of two plays about the siege, possibly in collaboration with the playwright, George Farquhar, who was actually born in Shipquay Street in Derry and although a child at the time of the siege must have been greatly influenced by the contemporary events.

His own death must have preyed upon Mitchelburne, because, in old age, he became very pious. He had a shed erected near a well in Gobnascale where he kept his coffin and used to go every morning to pray. The old governor is buried in the old Glendermott cemetery in the Waterside district, where, in 1836, the Honourable The Irish Society renovated his grave. It is a white marble altar tomb with inscriptions cut on all four sides and is surrounded by black railings. On one of these sides, it says "He was governor and commander in chief at the late memorable siege of Londonderry, in 1689, in defence of the Protestant interest, in the first year of the reign of King William of blessed memory". In view of this, it is therefore surprising that a Catholic cult grew up around Mitchelburne – at the site of the well in Gobnascale. Visitors to the well became convinced of the healing power of its waters and Mitchelburne acquired the status of its presiding "saint".

Dr A Gilfillen (1793–1838) was the naval surgeon on John Franklin's first Arctic expedition on HMS Trent. He was born at Gorticross on the outskirts of Derry and is buried in the family grave in the old Enagh Lough church near Strathfoyle. (His father appears to have died on the same day, 27 March 1838 but their cause of death is unknown.)

The disappearance of Franklin and his crews on the 1845 Arctic voyage to find the North-West Passage captured the imagination of the entire British Isles and was the subject of much speculation and newspaper coverage. The government financed many fruitless expeditions to try and locate them. As well as the more orthodox search parties, dozens of more bizarre offers of help were received. Lady Jane Franklin was inundated with accounts of visions and dreams from psychics, mediums and nutcases who maintained they knew her husband's whereabouts.

One of the letters she received was from a shipbuilder and surveyor of ships for the Board of Trade, Captain William Coppin, of Derry. His four-year-old daughter, **Louisa "Weesy"**

Coppin, (1845–1849) had died a few months previously but her "ghost" had since appeared to his wife and his other children several times. Under questioning about Lord Franklin, she had written on the wall the letters BS P.RI – NF, which Captain Coppin understood to mean the Barrow Strait, Prince Regent's Inlet, Newfoundland. Lady Franklin was convinced enough by the story of Miss Coppin's apparition that she raised yet more money to finance another search party under the command of Sir Francis Leopold McClintock of Dundalk to make one final attempt to find her husband. McClintock's voyage was successful – Franklin's ship and the bodies of the perished crew were found in Prince Regent's Inlet!

"Weesy" Coppin is buried in St Augustine's churchyard in Derry with a baby sister, Harriet, and her father although Captain Coppin's name does not appear on the stone. The grave is located near the railings of the churchyard on the side adjoining the Derry walls. It is a most attractive church and location, now thought to have been the site where St Columcille founded his early church.

The first grave on the left of the entrance into the churchyard of St Columb's Cathedral belongs to **William Hamilton** (1755–1793). Its explicit inscription tells us that:

"In his death, the cause of religion has to lament the loss of one of its ablest advocates, virtue one of its best supporters and learning one of its highest ornaments. He was assassinated at the house of Dr Waller at Sharon on the 2nd August 1793 where he fell a victim to the brutal fury of an armed banditti".

Reverend Hamilton had been appointed rector at Fanad in County Donegal where his activities as a local magistrate made him wildly unpopular. In March 1793, while he was staying at Sharon Glebe, the house was besieged by armed men and Hamilton and the wife of the local doctor were both murdered. Hamilton had been well-known too as a geologist and wrote a *Natural History of the Antrim Coast*, in particular about the Giant's Causeway. A feature of the Giant's Causeway, Hamilton's Seat, in fact, is named after him.

This practice of spelling out explicitly the circumstances of death can be seen on another memorial inside the cathedral to **Thomas Douglas Bateson**, another "upright, active and determined magistrate" and murder victim. Bateson was "murdered by Ribbonmen at Castleblaney in December 1851." The Ribbonmen were one of the many secret agrarian societies active at the time demanding land reform.

There is another memorial and lengthy tribute to **Captain John McNeil Boyd**, a native of Derry, "who in the hurricane of 9th Febuary 1861 sacrificed his own life in the noble act of saving the lives of others by obeying the never disregarded call to danger and to duty . . . the intrepid commander, the accomplished sailor, the warm friend and the consistent Christian." Captain Boyd is buried in St Patrick's Cathedral in Dublin. For the full story of how he met his death see the entry for Carrickbrennan graveyard in Dublin.

The wife of a former Bishop of Derry, **Mrs Cecil Frances Alexander** (1818–1895), is buried in the City Cemetery. She was the composer of many hymns, among them "All Things Bright and Beautiful", "Once in Royal David's City" and "There is a Green Hill Far Away". Her grave is marked by a simple white marble cross with the words:

> *Your daughters shall prophesy*
> *Your old men shall dream dreams*
> *Your young men shall see visions*

Four months after her death, her husband William Alexander was elected Archbishop of Armagh and Primate of All Ireland. He is buried in the same plot.

MAGHERA

In the confusion and terror in periods of insurrection, it was not always possible or politic for relatives to reclaim the remains of the executed which is why the location of their graves is often unknown. In the old graveyard in the church of St Lurach, Crewe Hill, near Maghera, there are two stones said to mark the graves of two United Irishmen, but only one of them is genuine. **Watty Graham** (d.1798), one of the local leaders of the United Irishmen, was hanged on a tree near the old church of St Lurach and is buried in the churchyard. One of his co-rebels, **Billy Cuddy**, was also hanged but local tradition claims that his body was cut down by his friends before he had finally expired. Billy revived and was smuggled out of the country to America. To deceive the authorities, however, his family and friends staged a mock funeral and had a weighted coffin buried in St Lurach's. There is still a stone marked "The Burying Place of William Cuddy".

DUNGIVEN

In the ruins of the twelfth-century Augustinian Priory outside Dungiven, there is the magnificent tomb of **Cooey-na-nGall O'Cahan** (d.1385). Despite weathering, this very old tomb is still splendid, one of the finest in the north, with the sculptured figures of six kilted gallowglass warriors on the front. Dungiven was the stronghold of the Gaelic chieftains the O'Cahans until, in the plantation of Ulster, their lands were confiscated and granted to the London Company of Skinners in 1609.

Three miles south of Dungiven in Banagher Church there is another ancient tomb – it looks like an early Christian oratory with its high-pitched roof but is actually a mortuary house, the reputed burial place of the founder of this church, **St Muireadach O'Heney**. There is another mortuary house or saint's grave at Bovevagh, the site of a pre-Norman church. It has a body-shaped cavity and a hole at one end where pilgrims could insert their hand to touch the relics!

SLAGHTAVERTY, NEAR GARVAGH

A strange tradition has attached itself to a dolmen near Garvagh called Slaghtaverty, or the monument of **Abhartach.** He was a dwarf who possessed magical powers which he exercised so maliciously on his local community that the chieftain had him killed and buried here upside down! The dolmen is on a hill about three miles south of Garvagh.

COUNTY DONEGAL

John Morley, Liberal MP and a former Chief Secretary for Ireland under Gladstone, described Gweedore as "one of the rudest and wildest spots in Her Majesty's dominions. I doubt if there is living in Her Majesty's Dominions a people living a harder life than the people of Gweedore." He was speaking in the aftermath of a shocking murder that had in turn followed upon large-scale evictions from the Olphert estates.

Irish tenant farmers led a precarious life. Their rents were not fixed and could be raised for any or no reason. If a farmer drained land, increased the number of lifestock he had or glazed a window of his house, the landlord rewarded his industry with a rent increase. And he could be summarily evicted, without notice, if the landlord decided he would prefer to devote the land to deer-stalking or sheep-farming. These evictions were carried out with a viciousness and lack of humanity that still takes the breath away. Wybrant Olphert, a landowner with huge tracts of land in Cloghaneely, Ballyconnell and part of Gweedore, has the dubious distinction of being the first to employ the battering ram to persuade his unwanted tenants to quit their cabins. Three graves in Donegal link a bloody episode in this period of history in Donegal.

BALLYSHANNON

According to the inscription on his tomb in St Anne's

graveyard, Mullaghnashee, Ballyshannon, **Inspector William Limrick Martin** was "foully murdered at Derrybeg Chapel Gweedore on Sunday 3rd Feb. 1889 in the 45th year of his age." Inspector Martin of the Royal Irish Constabulary had been supervising evictions from Wybrant Olphert's estate the previous day and had then travelled on to Gweedore where he was planning to arrest the parish priest, **Father James McFadden** (1842–1917). McFadden was an ardent champion of the people in their opposition to the landlords and had recently attended a meeting to establish a branch of the Land League at which he had declared, "I am the law in Gweedore". When the priest left the church after Mass, about eighty officers had surrounded the church grounds. Martin approached the priest with sword drawn, seized him by the collar and arrested him. In the fracas that ensued, Martin was fatally struck, with a length of paling.

Father McFadden was duly charged with the murder of the officer. The whole area was occupied by the military. Gunboats patrolled the coast to make sure no one could hide out on the off-shore islands. A curfew was imposed and men were arrested whether they had been at Mass that morning or not: finally thirty others were charged with murder along with Fr McFadden. The lengthy trial which followed ended abruptly when his co-defendants pleaded guilty on condition that Fr McFadden was liberated and that no prisoner be sentenced to death. In the event, they received sentences ranging from ten years' penal servitude to six months' hard labour. After the trial, the priest withdrew from such active campaigning and later became parish priest at Glenties where he is buried in the churchyard. **Wybrant Olphert** is buried on the old Ballyconnell estate, near Falcarragh alongside his horse. The elaborate monument of brass and black marble was erected by public subscription though not without vehement dissent from several quarters.

Another grave in the Ballyshannon graveyard reminds us

of an age when gentlemen resorted to pistols at dawn to sort out their differences, especially if a lady's honour was in question. After a night at the theatre which had been attended by many of the resident military personnel a quarrel broke out between a Lieutenant McGovern and a local attorney called George Henderson. Tempers flared. The challenge of a duel was thrown down and duly accepted. The duel took place on the riverside at Laputa the following morning and McGovern was killed outright. The tombstone over his grave was erected by his regiment with the following inscription:

*Returned to his native earth, here lieth all that was mortal of **Lieutenant Taaffe M'Govern**, late of Northumberland Regiment of Fencible Infantry. He fell in a duel on the 2nd March, 1802, in the 23rd year of his age. If the esteem and regard of his brother officers who have erected this stone to his memory could assist his soul in its flight to heaven, its ascent must have been rapid and its reception good.*

The poet **William Allingham** (1824–1889), is in the same Ballyshannon graveyard as the murdered Inspector Martin and the duellist McGovern. Allingham was brought up in Ballyshannon where his father was a bank manager. William Allingham also worked for the bank and as a customs officer before moving to England where he was friend and contemporary of Thackeray, Leigh Hunt, Tennyson and Rossetti. Like so many expatriates, Allingham did not settle down and kept moving back and forth between England and Ireland. He was cremated at Woking and his ashes buried in the Ballyshannon churchyard where his parents and other members of his family are also interred. His epitaph, written by himself, and read aloud at his cremation, was:

Body to purifying flame,
Soul to the Great Deep whence it came,
Leaving a song on earth below
An urn of ashes white as snow.

There is also a plaque on the Mall, a bronze bust in the

bank building where he had once worked and a marble tablet on Ballyshannon bridge.

GORTAHORK

Seven crew members of the British gunboat HMS *Wasp*, wrecked on 22 September 1884, lie together in a communal grave in St Anne's Church in Killult near Gortahork. The ship foundered on its journey to Tory to collect overdue rents or evict the islanders. Forty-eight sailors were drowned. Since the sea and weather conditions were fair, foul play was suspected. The islanders were accused of having turned off the lights of the lighthouse to lure the ship astray on to the rocks. They denied this. Others believed that they had caused the disaster by turning the Cloch Thoraí, the notorious cursing stones of Tory, on the ship. The rock where the ship perished is still known as "Feadán an Wasp". Other victims of the shipwreck are buried on Tory island; two others (Brewer and Sing) lie in the Church of Ireland churchyard at the crossroads in Bunbeg.

MAHERAGALLON

Protective head-gear might be in order for visitors to the old walled graveyard at Magheragallon, near Bunbeg. It is magnificently situated beside the Atlantic ocean, overlooking the islands, but has now been completely surrounded by a golf course. Magheragallon has special significance for me as many of my own relatives are buried here, a motley crew of hoteliers, politicians and teachers.

Against one of its drystone walls is the grave and monument of "An Piobaire Mór", **Turlough MacSweeney**, the piper. MacSweeney is an example of how fortunes could be reversed in Ireland. This itinerant piper who lived in a small thatched cottage on the Hill estate at Gweedore was a direct lineal descendant of the McSweeney chieftains of Doe Castle who had lost their land and titles in 1690.

In 1893 Turlough MacSweeney represented Ireland at the Chicago World Fair and spent six months there giving daily performances. Declining the offer of a handsome salary to stay in America he retorted, "Whether do you think I would like to die – in the Land of Saints or the Land of Snakes." He died in 1916. The cross and monument over his grave were erected by his children, ironically all of them by then living in America. Everybody in Magheragallon is buried with their backs to the sea – except for An Piobaire Mór whose grave faces the opposite direction. Locals say that he is still facing his audience.

There is a striking grave slab at the entrance to the Catholic church in Killybegs of one of the piper's illustrious ancestors, the chieftain **Niall Mor McSwyne** who died in 1524. It is elaborately carved with a representation of the chief himself, a deer, wolfhound, horse, lizard along with a number of other symbols and interlaced work.

DUNGLOE

Paddy "the Cope" Gallagher (1873–1964), the founder of the co-operative movement in Donegal, is buried in Dungloe. Barefooted and with nothing but a couple of shirts and some thread and buttons, he started work at ten years of age when he was sent to a hiring fair. Later he worked in Scotland and England as a labourer and miner, before returning with enough money to buy a smallholding in Cleendra in the Rosses. In 1906, against fierce opposition from the local "gombeen men", he founded the Templecrone Co-operative Society to buy meal and staple goods like tea and sugar. The story of how the cooperative flourished is told in his autobiography *My Story* which he wrote in 1939. It recounts how the "cope" exported knitted goods and tweed, built the pier at Dungloe, set up a glove factory, and even supplied electricity to the town. Gallagher is buried in Dungloe Catholic churchyard.

A tablet on the wall of Dungloe church is dedicated to **William Smyth** of Roshine Lodge, Burtonport who died of typhus fever in 1901 at the age of forty-two. Dr Smyth had contracted the disease by personally coming to the rescue of a stricken family called Gallagher who were being boycotted by their neighbours on Arranmore Island. The doctor decided they needed to be taken to hospital but since none of the islanders was prepared to help them for fear of contamination, he himself bought a boat and rowed out to the island to bring them to the mainland himself. He fell ill and died a few days later.

The tablet records how he died trying to prevent the spread of disease and quotes Robert Browning: *"One who never turned his back but/marched breast forward/Never doubted clouds would break/Never dreamed, though right were/ Worsted, wrong would triumph/Held, we fall to rise, are baffled to/fight better, sleep to wake."*

ARRANMORE ISLAND

Arranmore Island was the scene of another tragedy when, late on the evening of 9 November 1935, a group of migrant workers returning from Scotland were drowned within sight of their homes. Twenty people were on board the boat which ran onto the rocks half a mile from harbour at a place called Béal an Éilín. Nobody saw or heard anything – the islanders may have assumed the boat had not sailed from Burtonport – and it was not until early the following morning that a man saw the upturned boat. There was only one survivor. Those who died are buried in a communal grave on Arranmore. There is now a frequent ferry service to the island.

RATHMULLAN PRIORY

In 1811 England was at war with France and its navy was patrolling and blockading the whole coast of Europe. Lough Swilly was at the time a naval station. On the night of 4

December 1811, the British warship, HMS *Saldanha*, part of the fleet fighting in the war against Napoleon, was shipwrecked in atrocious storms at Ballymastocker Bay (now the site of the Port Salon hotel) with the loss of all 300 men. The ship's young captain, **William Pakenham** (1782–1811), a son of the second Lord Longford, had recently returned from engagements in La Corunna in Spain. It is said that on receipt of his sealed orders to put to sea, he had a premonition of his own death, predicting that if the *Saldanha* was sent to Inishowen, he would perish, and so it happened. Captain Pakenham's large railed tomb stands in a splendid location in the grounds of the old priory overlooking the sea.

A curious postscript to this disaster is that a green parrot was captured in Burt several months after the wreck. Around its neck it had a medallion inscribed with the name of the ship *Saldanha*. Whatever became of it afterwards is not known.

The *Saldanha* was clearly not blessed with good luck, for near Pakenham's grave, beneath a flat stone, are the bodies of eight seamen who drowned in an earlier tragedy in January of the same year when their small boat capsized in heavy seas as they were ferrying fresh water to the ship.

FAHAN, INISHOWEN

In 1811, the same year that the *Saldanha* perished, another British warship, HMS *Endymion*, was in Lough Swilly. Its muster book records that midshipman **Horatio Nelson** was sick on 2 September and the captain recommended a "run on shore". The owner of Fahan House, Rear Admiral William Heath was prevailed upon to look after him. Despite careful nursing, his condition continued to deteriorate and Horatio Nelson, "an amiable youth . . . breathed his last at Fahan House in the eighteenth year of his age" and is buried in the old parish church of Fahan.

Although there is little evidence of kinship with Admiral Horatio Nelson, the young midshipman was from Burnham

Thorpe in Norfolk, Nelson's birth-place and was believed locally to be his nephew. It is certainly interesting that his captain should have been so concerned that he should have a "run on shore" and that so distinguished a family should take him in. Perhaps on the other hand he was, as his tombstone says just "an amiable youth – Could friendship have prolonged his days he had lived."

A later resident at Fahan House was the pioneering nurse, **Agnes Jones** (1832–1868). She trained at St Thomas's Hospital in London with Florence Nightingale and was then sent to the Brownlow Hill Workhouse in Liverpool, an institution that housed upwards of 1,200 paupers. Here, as Florence Nightingale wrote in the magazine *Good Words* in June 1868, Jones became "the pioneer of workhouse nursing," the first person to introduce trained nurses in a workhouse infirmary. In less than three years, "she reduced one of the most disorderly hospital populations in the world to something like Christian discipline such as the police themselves wondered at." In February 1867 Jones herself wrote of her experiences there: "I sometimes wonder if there is a worse place on earth – but I never regret coming and I never wish to give it up." The following year she contracted typhus fever and died. Nurse Jones was a friend of William Alexander who had been rector of Fahan and of his wife, the hymn-writer Frances Alexander. When her body was brought back to Donegal for burial, Alexander, then the Bishop of Derry, wrote the poem which is inscribed on the memorial inside the church.

> *. . . Proudly as men heroic ashes claim*
> *We ask'd to have thy fever-stricken frame,*
> *And lay it in our grass beside our foam*
> *Till Christ the Healer calls his Healers home.*

There is also a memorial stained glass window with a portrait of Agnes Jones in the Anglican Cathedral in Liverpool. Altnagelvin Hospital Nurse Training School in Derry is named after her.

During the first World War, on 26 January 1917, the Inishowen coast witnessed yet another tragedy when a German submarine torpedoed the steel ship, HMS *Laurentic*. Sixty-eight of the victims were buried in a mass grave beside the Church of Ireland in Fahan. Many bodies were never recovered. Only twelve officers and just 100 men survived. The incident occurred in the very early morning when most of the ship's crew were sleeping so there was no opportunity to man life-boats.

MUFF

The snatching of fresh corpses from their graves for sale to surgeons was a new and alarming development in the early nineteenth century. Two of the most notorious practitioners were William Burke, a Corkman, and William Hare from Derry, though they carried out their grisly business in Edinburgh. However, body-snatchers, known colloquially as "sack-em-ups" or "resurrection men" were at work all over Ireland too. Desperate measures were taken to protect the newly dead, including encasing the coffin in an iron cage – one of these coffin guards can be seen in the Ulster Museum.

In 1829, the year that William Burke was hanged, **John Gwyn**, the Derry grocer and benefactor of the Gwyn Institute (he bequeathed the huge sum of £40,000 for the education and upkeep of orphan boys in Derry) was so appalled by the prospect of his body being stolen and mutilated after his death that he left very specific instructions in his will about his interment.

"It is my wish that my remains should be kept unburied for three nights; the grave to be ten feet deep, with a quantity of wheatstraw, well drawn, put above the coffin, to prevent resurrection-men from disturbing my grave; and it is also my wish that Thomas Doherty, of Muff, should employ three or four trusty men to keep watch in the churchyard for some time after interment – expenses to be paid by my Executors."

One presumes that his wishes were respected when he was buried in Muff graveyard. The practice of body-snatching eventually stopped with the Anatomy Act in 1832 which permitted the supply of bodies for dissection, often those of executed criminals.

INVER

In the old Inver graveyard, near Mountcharles, there is a badly weathered and broken limestone slab dedicated to the memory of "**Thomas Nesbitt**, of Kilmacredon, who departed this life on 15 Dec. 1801, aged 79." Thomas Nesbitt was the inventor of the harpoon swivel gun. For some years in the 1760s, Nesbitt had developed Ireland's only professional and successful whaling fleet, sailing out of the port of Killybegs where whales appeared in great numbers each spring. Despite disastrous losses during their first seasons, it attracted government subsidies and went on to do reasonably well. However we regard the demand in the nineteenth century for whale oil and whalebone today, Nesbitt's invention was way ahead of its time.

STRANORLAR, BALLYBOFEY

The role played by **Isaac Butt** (1813–1879), in Irish politics is often overlooked. The famine and, in particular, British neglect of Ireland during those years, horrified Butt and changed his natural political leanings. He wrote at the time that even to profess belief in the existence of a formidable potato blight was enough to be branded a radical. The calamity of the famine, he argued, ought to be regarded as an imperial one and if the Empire was not prepared to concede help, then Ireland had every right to demand a separate legislative existence. As a lawyer, he defended William Smith O'Brien and others after the Fenian rising in 1848 and continued to defend Fenians although it was very much against his financial interests to do so and he was once imprisoned for debt. In 1870 he founded and was leader of the Home Rule movement until succeeded by the more radical Parnell. He is buried in Stranorlar.

BOGS AND THEIR BURIED SECRETS

A great part of Donegal is covered in peat bog, an evocative landscape with its own distinctive ecology, its particular flora of heather, bog cotton and sphagnum moss. Turf is still in common use as a fuel so that the county even smells unlike the rest of the country. But peat has another particular property: it acts as a preservative for objects lost or buried in it, particularly items made of leather, wood, fabric – and bone!

In the Bog of Allen, wooden roadways, two thousand years old, have been uncovered. Ancient boats have been unearthed as have silver chalices, perhaps dropped by marauding Vikings or carefully hidden by fleeing monks. Men working on bogs saving the turf still occasionally come across tubs of butter, buried centuries ago in wicker or wooden containers and for some reason never recovered. The stumps of ancient trees, bog oak, are frequently uprooted.

But bogs can be sinister places too, with their bog pools and marshy unstable ground where a stranger might easily go astray and die alone and undiscovered. The most interesting discoveries underneath the peat are the bog bodies, about eighty of which have been found since 1750. Some of these bog bodies were clearly buried deliberately.

In 1978 a farmer cutting turf found one of these bodies in the upland bog of Meenbraddan near Inver. It was the naked body of a woman who had been carefully wrapped in a coarse blanket or cloak. Her hair, eyelashes, eyebrows and fingernails were still in good condition but the acidity of the peat had stained her skin dark brown. Carbon dating and analyis of the cloak revealed that she had been lying there since the late Middle Ages, sometime between the eleventh and fifteenth centuries. There was no visible cause of death. Unfortunately the same cannot be said about another Donegal woman whose uncorrupted body was discovered in September 1840 in Ballykinard bog, also on the Fanad peninsula. She was dressed in a flannel petticoat and wore a scarlet handkerchief around her head. Her limbs were still elastic, her features perfectly formed – even the few smallpox she had were still visible – but her throat was cut. At the inquest which followed the discovery of the body, she was identified as **Betty Thompson**, the wife of Owen McSwine, who had disappeared in unexplained circumstances thirty years earlier. No one was convicted of her murder.

Yet another bog body which can still be seen in the National Museum in Dublin was originally found buried three metres deep in a bog near Castleblakeney in County Galway in 1821. A contemporary account of the discovery was written by the antiquarian George Petrie. The body was of a man, naked except for a deerskin leather cape which was tied around his neck with twisted sally rods. Two long wooden stakes by his side apparently pinned him to the ground. For some time after the find, the body became a local curiosity and was dug up again several times to be shown to sightseers. It eventually was passed on to the National Museum where it has been studied and carbon-dated. There is no doubt that the bog-man lived in the Iron Age and was the subject of a ritual burial, perhaps even a ritual killing since the sally rods around his neck would seem to indicate that he was strangled, a similar fate to that of the Iron Age bog-men found in Germany and Denmark.

DOWN

DOWNPATRICK

Three of Ireland's greatest saints are buried in the grounds of Down Cathedral in Downpatrick, allegedly re-interred together here by the Norman John de Courcy. Lying under a huge monolith of granite from the Mourne mountains are the patron saint of Ireland, **Saint Patrick** (c.390–c.461), **Saint Brigid** (c.525) and **Saint Colmcille** (521–597).

From *The Confession of St Patrick*, we know that Patrick was a Roman Briton, the son of a Christian called Calpurnius, probably from a settlement on Hadrian's Wall. As a youth, he was kidnapped by an Irish raiding party and spent several years in Ireland as a slave before escaping and becoming a priest. He had visions in which he heard Irish voices begging him to return which tradition tells us he did in 432. He stayed until his death, converting the Irish to Christianity, "a stranger and an exile for the love of God". His first church is believed to be at Saul, just outside Downpatrick, on land given to him by a local chief, Dichu, his first convert.

Less is known about Saint Brigid, Ireland's premier female saint whose feast day is celebrated on 1 February, though we do know that she founded a religious house at Kildare.

Saint Colmcille was born in Gartan, County Donegal. After what was probably one of the first but not the last disputes in Ireland over copyright, Colmcille went into exile because of a quarrel about a copy of a psaltery that he had

219

made without permission. The dispute was settled by the high king's judgment: "To every cow its calf, and to every book its copy." Colmcille did not accept the judgment and in the battle that ensued many lives were lost. In atonement for these deaths, he exiled himself to Iona where he founded the island monastery. Iona also claims to be his burial place.

In the porch of the cathedral, on the north wall, look for the monument to **Oliver Cromwel**: no, not that Oliver Cromwell but a son of the Earl of Ardglas and distant relative of the Lord Protector. He died in 1668. Cromwell's Irish connections did not seem, as any Irish person will testify, to have made him sentimental about the place.

Thomas Russell (1767–1803) was hanged in Downpatrick at the gateway to Down County Gaol (now the Down County Museum) and is buried in the grounds of the Church of Ireland parish church at the bottom of the hill. Together with Henry Joy McCracken and Samuel Neilson, Russell was one of the main leaders of the United Irishmen in Down and Antrim. However, he was arrested in 1796 and was imprisoned in Dublin and Fort George so took no part in the 1798 rebellion. On his release in 1802, he went to Paris where he met Robert Emmet. They agreed to stage simultaneous uprisings in Belfast and Dublin. When Emmet's rebellion failed and Russell failed to get the support he needed in the North, he returned to Dublin where he was re-arrested by Major Sirr (see St Werburgh's, Dublin). Mary-Ann McCracken, who was in love with him, attempted to bribe his jailers and spring him but was unsuccessful. He was then brought back to Downpatrick for trial, found guilty of treason, hanged and decapitated. It was Mary Ann McCracken who later erected his gravestone which just reads "The grave of Russell, 1803". The death of this romantic idealist with his "strange up-country talk" is also remembered in a popular ballad *"The Man from God-Knows-Where"*:

Then he bowed his head to the swinging rope,

Whiles I said 'Please God' to his dying hope
And 'Amen' to his dying prayer
That the Wrong would cease and the Right prevail,
For the man that they hanged at Downpatrick gaol
Was the Man from God-Knows-Where

RADEMON

Rev William Neilson (1774–1821) is buried in the family tomb in Rademon six miles north of Downpatrick. This was a most unusual man, a Presbyterian minister who published a pioneering textbook, *Introduction to the Irish Language*. At that time in pre-famine Ireland, Irish was widely spoken in Presbyterian as well as Catholic congregations. Neilson was apparently very fond of preaching in Irish despite being arrested once for doing so; far from being subversive, however, Neilson was a loyal subject of the crown. Later when he became Head of Classics at the Belfast Academical Institution, he insisted that students should also study Irish since knowledge of the language was "highly important to the philological scholar and the antiquarian". It is said that 15,000 people attended his funeral.

SEAFORDE

Amanda McKitterick Ros (1860–1939), a formidable woman widely held to be "the world's worst novelist", is buried in the little graveyard at Seaforde with her second husband, Tom Rodgers. Amanda was so bizarre a writer that she attracted a cult following in Oxford and her books were republished at the insistence of Aldous Huxley. She would appear to have been unaware of the real reason for her "success". She was very touchy about criticism and composed scathing replies to her critics: "Their bayonets of bastard sheen with their scurrilous punctures of jealousy jadery affect neither the book nor its author." On another occasion she took issue with the "stale spuings, the ungrammatical effortless efforts of a criticising crowdrop." Corpses held a morbid fascination for her as her immortal *"Lines on Westminster Abbey"* shows:

> *Holy Moses! Take a look!*
> *Flesh decayed in every nook,*
> *Some rare bits of brain lie here*
> *Mortal loads of beef and beer . . .*

BANBRIDGE

Banbridge was the home of **Captain Francis Lawdon Moira Crozier** (1796–1848), one of several forgotten explorers from Northern Ireland. He is recognised as the discoverer of the North-West passage, the sea route linking the Atlantic and the Pacific. Since he perished on the last of his Arctic voyages, he does not have a grave but there is a monument to him in Church Square opposite the house where he lived. It is a huge structure with flying buttresses and four polar bears. On his last expedition with Franklin, they had discovered the North-West passage but their ship became ice-bound. Assuming the command when Franklin died, Crozier attempted to reach land but tragically, with provisions running low, they all perished. Their bodies were not found until 1859 when Lady Franklin financed an expedition to search for them. Interestingly, there were allegations at the time from Eskimos that they had found the bodies and that there were clear indications of cannibalism from the mutilated state of the corpses and the contents of cooking pots. These reports were vehemently denied by the *Times* who thundered "All savages are liars." (For other Franklin expedition connections, see Gilfillen and Coppin, Derry.)

KILKEEL

Another pioneering explorer, and an Ulsterman, is **Francis Rawdon Chesney** (1789–1872), the "father of the Suez canal" who is buried in Kilkeel. In 1829, he explored Egypt and Syria and showed that a Suez canal was a practicable proposition. He went on to map out the feasibility of a new route to India, through Syria and the Persian Gulf, even transporting two steamboats across the desert and navigating the Euphrates to the Persian Gulf (though one of the ships was wrecked in a storm with the loss of twenty lives). This route was also deemed realisable but was never carried out. Chesney had had an action-packed life – he was commissioned as a sub-lieutenant in the infantry at the age of nine and first saw active service against the United Irishmen in 1798.

NEWRY

Buried in Newry, in the Unitarian First Presbyterian Church in Old Meetinghouse Green by the High Street, is **John Mitchel** (1818–1875). A Young Irelander, he became editor of the influential newspaper *The Nation*. Mitchel was deeply affected by the famine and became convinced of the need for militant opposition to British rule. He was convicted of sedition and sentenced to transportation, first to Bermuda, then to Van Diemen's Land.

In 1853, he managed to escape to the United States where he remained for several years, mostly in the southern states where he defended slavery. "Negro slavery is the best state of existence for the negro and the best for his master," he wrote in his autobiographical *Jail Journal or Five Years in British Prisons* (1856). Proponents of liberty and equality are not always without blind spots. Mitchel remained in America until 1874, moving frequently because as he wrote, "since that banishment from my own country and the sudden severing of all the roots that bound me to the soil . . . I am conscious of a certain vagabond propensity." He returned to Ireland in that year and was elected MP for Tipperary though ineligible to take his seat as he was an undischarged felon.

There is a statue of Mitchel outside St Colman's Park, just a short walk from the church.

BANGOR

In Bangor Abbey, a memorial to the memory of **Archibel Wilson** (d.1798) is well worth looking for. Wilson was accused of treason and hanged as a United Irishman at Bangor Pier but went to his death protesting his innocence. The wonderfully mis-spelt inscription which Wilson composed for himself while awaiting trial in prison reads (and is even better if you can read it aloud in an Ulster accent):

> *Morn Not deer frends tho Im no more*
> *Tho I was martred your eys before*
> *I am not dead but do Sleep hear*
> *And yet once more I will apeer*
> *That is when time will be no more*
> *when thel be Judged who falsly sore*
> *and them that Judged will Judged be*
> *Whither Just or onJust then thel see*
> *Purpere deer frends for that grate day*
> *when death dis sumance you away*
> *I will await ayoul with due care*
> *in heven with Joy to meet you there.*

GREYABBEY

On the Ards peninsula, in the tranquil ruins of the Cistercian Greyabbey founded in 1193 by Alfreca, the wife of the Norman John de Courcy, there are a number of fascinating graves and memorials to the Montgomerys who were given the lands of the abbey after the dissolution of the monasteries in 1541. They were an important Protestant settler family who lived in exciting times. Here lies **James Montgomery** "by pirates shot" when in 1651 he was returning from battle in Scotland. There is the Montgomery who was drowned when his ship perished on the Alacranes Reef in Mexico and another who was three times wounded in battle in the Napoleonic and Peninsular wars, was present at the occupation of Paris and later died of his wounds.

In the adjoining graveyard there is a partly vandalised grave of another United Irishman, **Rev James Porter**, minister of the First Presbyterian Church at Grey Abbey who was hanged, drawn and quartered on the orders of the Marquis of Londonderry in July 1798. Porter had been a tutor to the Marquis' family at one time but that did not stop him lampooning him frequently in the press and highlighting the poverty and injustices suffered by Lord Londonderry's tenants. His lordship had him arrested on a spurious charge of intercepting His Majesty's Mail, a capital offence.

In Mr and Mrs Hall's account of their journey around Ireland in 1842, they recount a meeting in this churchyard with "two grey-headed Presbyterians" at the grave of another United Irishman, the **Rev Archibald Warwick** (d.1798), the charismatic Presbyterian minister of this parish. One of these old men had witnessed the execution of the minister on a nearby hill. He tells the Halls " . . . if (Warwick) had been less engaging he would have been more fortunate for then he could not have been regarded as an object of such danger to the government, but as one to whom they would gladly have extended mercy for the sake of conciliation . . . " Thousands of people assembled from all parts of the country to take their farewell of him. As the minister mounted the gallows, the assembled crowds "burst forth in a loud hymn and in that burst of heavenly music he passed away."

There is a third United Irishman's grave here too: **Alexander Byers** (1754–1798), killed in battle in a street in Ballynahinch on the evening after the rebels were routed from Windmill Hill, the site of the main local confrontation between the rebel army and the militia.

BALLYCREEN, NEAR BALLYNAHINCH

The decisive defeat of the insurgents at Ballynahinch put an end to the rebellion in the North. Hundreds were killed. The remainder fled in panic with the militia in hot pursuit. All over County Down, summary court-martials, executions, plunder and murder were commonplace. General Harry Munro, the reluctant commander of the rebel troops, taking refuge in a farm near Dromore, was betrayed, taken prisoner, court-martialled and executed in Lisburn on a temporary gallows erected in front of his own draper shop. Many others, like **Betsy Gray**, the beautiful heroine of several 1798 ballads, died at the hands of vengeful yeomen.

Fleeing from the battle-site, Betsy Gray, who had carried the green flag into battle, her brother **George Gray** and **William Boal** were seized and killed by local yeomen militia at Ballycreen about a mile and a half outside Ballynahinch on the Belfast road. They were buried there together in a shallow grave. Although unmarked and on private ground, the site became a place of pilgrimage in the ensuing years.

Almost one hundred years later, in 1896, a descendant of Miss Gray sought permission from the owner of the land to erect a monument on the site of the grave. With the approach of the centenary of the 1798 rebellion and the possibility of the granting of Home Rule to Ireland, the political climate in the province was highly charged and the erection of the memorial stone proved too much to take in some quarters. The appropriation of the grave by Nationalists was deemed "a piece of unwarrantable presumption" as the local newspaper reported.

On Sunday 1 May 1898, there was a violent confrontation between Nationalists and Orangemen at Ballycreen "which a strong body of police who were present do not seem to have been able to prevent". The headstone, surrounding railings and the wreaths placed on the grave were destroyed.

In J McCoy's account, Betsy Gray, *Ulster's Joan of Arc* (1987), it was stated that the grave had not been restored and the little that remained of the knocked-over headstone had been chipped away by souvenir hunters.

DROMORE

Bishop Jeremy Taylor (1613–1667) lies in a vault in Dromore Cathedral. Bishop Taylor was chaplain to Charles I and was imprisoned for some time in 1645 after the defeat of the Royalists in the English Civil War.

After the Restoration in 1660, he was appointed Bishop of Down and Connor and set about rebuilding the cathedral at Dromore to replace the medieval one burnt down in 1641 by Cromwell. He met with a great deal of hostility from the presbyterians in the diocese and for some time thirty-six churches were declared vacant because the ministers would not recognise his jurisdiction. He wrote: "I would rather be a poor curate in a village church than a bishop over such intolerable persons." His devotional books, *Rules and Exercises of Holy Living* and *Holy Dying* were extremely popular, going into many editions, and are still in use. He died of fever in Lisburn.

MAGHERALLY

The writer and scholar, **Helen Waddell** (1889–1965) is buried in Magherally parish church. Born in Tokyo of Ulster parents, she was educated in Belfast and later at Somerville College, Oxford. Her books included *Lyrics from the Chinese* (1915) and *Medieval Latin Lyrics* (1929) but she is best remembered now as the author of *Peter Abelard* (1933), the well-loved story of Abelard and Heloise, which went into more than thirty editions and was widely translated. She lived in London for many years where she was Vice-President of the Irish Literary Society and had a wide circle of literary friends including George Russell, WB Yeats, Virginia Woolf and Max Beerbohm. Her brother Samuel Waddell (1878–1967) was the playwright and actor, Rutherford Mayne, who wrote for the Abbey Theatre in Dublin and helped to found the Ulster Literary Theatre.

KILBRONEY

Dolmens and ancient tumuli are often called "giants' graves" but here, in the small graveyard in Kilbroney, about a mile outside Rostrevor, is the grave of a real Irish giant, **Patrick Murphy** (1834–1862). He is reputed to have been well over eight feet in height. Murphy spent years touring the world exhibiting himself at fairs, turning his freakish stature to advantage, but died in Marseilles while still a young man. His body was brought home to be buried in his native village.

FERMANAGH

Fermanagh is the county of strange stones. Two of the strangest, although not gravestones, deserve their place here for they stand in the old Caldragh churchyard on Boa Island. The two-faced Janus figures have large triangular heads with huge eyes, pointed beards, and a sort of stoup or hollow in between the two faces. Unique in Ireland, this style of stone-carving probably dates from about the third century BC, examples of the art of the La Tène culture. The smaller one, less well preserved, has one bulging eye, possibly a representation of Badhbha, the one-eyed hag of war, Celtic goddess of both destruction and creation. In any case Boa island, (pronounced Bow), which can be reached via a causeway, takes its name from this goddess. They are strange powerful images, all the more so for their incongruous setting.

The Bishop's Stone in Killadeas churchyard may well have been of the same pagan period but has been "Christianised". It is a crook-shaped standing stone, showing the figure of a walking man carrying a crozier and bell, these last two symbols probably additions to an earlier carving. Another monument here is a stone slab with a raised circle and a carved cross. On its side there are rows of scooped out hollows and there are suggestions that this too was a pagan artefact possibly related to the worship of the Earth Mother but absorbed and adapted by the new Christians.

CASTLECALDWELL

There is an enigmatic plaque at the entry to the Castlecaldwell Forest park near Belleek.

It is inscribed :

Beware ye fiddlers of ye fiddler's fate
Nor tempt the deep lest you repent too late
Ye ever have been deemed to water foes
Then shun ye lake till it with whiskey floes
On firm land only exercise your skill
There you may play and safely drink your fill
DDD

"This is to the memory of **Denis McCabe**, the fiddler, who fell out of the St Patrick's barge which belonged to Sir James Caldwell, Baronet and Count of Milan, and was drowned off this point August ye 13th 1770." There is some doubt as to whether the DDD means, Denis Died Drunk or Drink Drowned Denis.

ENNSIKILLEN

The Great War Memorial on Belmore Street was erected in memory of the soldiers who died in the tragedy of the First World War. On Remembrance Day 1987, the tragedy was compounded when the IRA planted a bomb here which exploded just as people were gathering for the memorial service. Eleven people were killed, many more injured. Among the dead was the nurse **Marie Wilson**, daughter of a local businessman **Gordon Wilson** (1927–1995). In the aftermath of her murder, Gordon Wilson's grief and his lack of bitterness towards her killers moved and inspired the world. Interviewed the following morning, he described how they had been buried together under six feet of rubble and how she had fallen silent after telling him she loved him. He went on "I have lost my daughter but I bear no ill will, I bear no grudge." Later he was to write in *Marie: A Story from*

Enniskillen (1990): "I still pray for the bombers and I continue to bear them no ill-will. Better men than I have wrestled with the whole concept of forgiveness and have failed . . . the last word rests with God . . . All I can do is to continue not to think evil or malicious thoughts about these people and to go on bearing them no ill-will." Gordon Wilson died in Enniskillen in 1995 and was buried in Breandrum graveyard, the town's main cemetery, with his daughter.

William Scott (1913–1989), the painter, is also buried in Breandrum. Born into a large family impoverished by the premature death of his father, his first art teacher was **Kathleen Bridle** (also buried in Breandrum). During the Second World War, he joined the British Army as a war artist. At first he gained a reputation for his still life paintings, "finding the mystery in the commonplace" but his work became increasingly abstract. He exhibited all over the world, from Venice to São Paolo, New York to London. I remember as a child in 1962 being taken to see a controversial William Scott mural which had been commissioned for the newly opened Altnagelvin Hospital in Derry. It was the first modern civic piece of art in the city and attracted hordes of weekend visitors, not all of whom could have been described as admirers.

BALLINAMALLARD

Margaret *"Orange Peggy"* **Elliot** (1783–1891) was a well-known personality in Fermanagh. Born on the island of Trasna (there are almost one hundred islands on the Lower Erne), she was christened on the 12 July wrapped up in an Orange flag and remained all her long life a staunch loyalist. The headstone over her grave is erected to: "Margaret Elliot, popularly known as Queen of Trasna and familiarly as Orange Peggy, who died 10th August 1891. Regretted not only by the Protestants of Fermanagh, but by all classes who for generations had learned to respect her." She was 108 years old. She is buried on the churchyard on the hill at Magheracross, near Ballinamallard.

Her husband and two sons are buried beside her – she had witnessed their drowning many years earlier in a sudden lake storm. Her grand-daughter is reputed to have always dressed in orange except for green stockings so that she could stamp on the colour of the opposition!

COLEBROOKE

Sir Basil Brooke (1888–1973), First Viscount Brookeborough, was actively involved in the politics of Northern Ireland almost from its inception and so can rightly be thought of as one of its key architects. Educated at Sandhurst, he was awarded the Military Cross and the Croix de Guerre in the First World War and was elected Unionist MP for Fermanagh in 1929. A wealthy landowner of estates in Fermanagh, when appointed Minister of Agriculture in 1933, he sacked all his Catholic workers to set an example for others. Having served in other ministries, he became Prime Minister in 1943 and held the position until 1963, during which time he contrived to avoid official contact with Roman Catholics and trade unionists. He was completely opposed to the liberalising policies of Captain Terence O'Neill who succeeded him as Prime Minister and to rapprochement with the Republic of Ireland. He died in his home in Colebrook 18 August 1973 and is buried there.

MONAGHAN

INNISKEEN

I expect the poet **Patrick Kavanagh** (1904–1967) may well be turning in his grave with the disputatious goings-on surrounding his final resting-place. He is buried in Inniskeen graveyard with his wife Katherine (1928–1989) whom he had married scarcely a year before his death. The inscription reads:

> *For we must record*
> *Love's mystery without claptrap*
> *Snatch out of time*
> *the passionate transitory.*

Originally stepping stones had been laid across the grave with the inscription: "There were stepping stones across a stream. Part of my life was there. The happiest part." However, these have now been re-laid on another "grave" in the garden of the house in the village of Mucker two kilometres away where Kavanagh had grown up with his brother Peter. A small teak cross is inscribed "And pray for him who walked apart on the hills loving life's miracle."

Both sites commemorate a man who had asked for "no hero-courageous tomb – just a canal bank seat for the passer-by" and this he has duly got too, on the banks of the Grand Canal near Baggot Street in Dublin.

ANNAGHMAKERRIG

The theatrical producer and director, **Sir William Tyrone**

Guthrie (1900–1971), is buried in the family plot in the grounds of Aghabog church a couple of miles away from his old family home at Annaghmakerrig. Guthrie was a towering figure in the theatrical world, both physically (he was 6ft 5") and metaphorically. His career spanned the globe, from running the Old Vic in London to establishing the Shakespeare Festival Theater in Stratford, Ontario, and founding the Guthrie Theater in Minneapolis. One of his greatest legacies could well be considered the Tyrone Guthrie Centre at Annaghmakerrig, the home he bequeathed as a working retreat for writers, musicians and artists. A large handsome house full of books and paintings set on the shores of a lake, it has been a temporary haven for a tide of grateful artists since it opened in 1981.

TYRONE

The gravestones in any churchyard represent only a fraction of the people buried there. Only the relatively better off had marked graves and the further you go back in time the less survives. Mediaeval monuments were rarely inscribed and the dissolution of monasteries led to the destruction not only of the interiors of abbeys and churches but to the wholesale vandalism of tombs and monuments. There are constant disappearances – many unusual stones that I read about in early twentieth century archaeological journals have already vanished without trace and there are constant casualties when churches are being "renovated".

When seeking out the burial places of ancestors it is salutary to remember that many interments were not recorded and this was not always the fault of a clergyman failing to keep his books in order. In the seventeenth and eighteenth centuries, families often buried their dead in secret to avoid paying burial fees. In Tyrone the 1754 records for Donagheady parish declare: "the reason so few burials are entered is an indecent custom of interring without sending to the minister to attend – that the papist should always, and the Presbyterians generally, omit it is not to be wondered; but it is astonishing that those who are of the Established Church should choose to bury their deceased friends like dogs".

DONAGHMORE

Rev George Walker (1618–1690), joint governor of the city of Derry during the 1689 siege, would doubtless have known all about people being buried like dogs since hundreds of victims of the siege had to be hurriedly buried in back-yards under a thin layer of dirt. Writing fifty years after the siege had ended, a Derry annalist, Robert Simpson could write:

In almost every part of the Island of Derry, both within and without the city, trenches full of human remains have been discovered, and single skeletons have been found. In clearing out the premises for the Gas Works, we have seen collected a vast heap of skulls and bones; and about five years ago, in clearing out a small inclosure, not far from Butcher's gate, once the scene of great actions, and adjoining the premises occupied by the first Presbyterian Meeting-house, a long trench was opened, out of which a dozen of skulls were raised; and from the regularity and sound appearance of the teeth, they seemed to us to have been those of young men who fell in the Siege: the remains were taken to manure a field of turnips! (Oh! Shades of our heroic ancestors!)

Governor Walker is buried in the Castlecaulfield church in the parish of Donaghmore where he had served as rector. As the siege had become more entrenched after the escape of the "traitor" Lundy, Walker was elected joint governor with Colonel Henry Baker (see St Columb's Cathedral, Derry). Together they organised the defences of the city, mounting guns on the tower of the cathedral and along the city walls. Governor Walker's graphic account of conditions within the besieged city still makes harrowing reading, but in time-honoured Irish fashion, his role as hero came under severe criticism once the siege had ended with allegations of corruption and cowardice from the Presbyterian minister, John Mackenzie.

The following year, Walker joined King William and his army on their arrival at Carrickfergus and accompanied them on their way south to confront King James at the Battle of the Boyne. He was killed by a stray bullet during the battle on 12 July 1690 and was first buried there at the battle-field. In 1703 his "still inconsolable" widow Isabella had his remains disinterred and taken back to Donaghmore for re-burial in his old church though doubts remain about their authenticity. In 1838 when the church was undergoing repairs, the oak casket was dug up and examined. There was a skull, two arm bones and two thigh bones, both of which appeared to be the same leg and so could not both have belonged to Walker.

The monument on the wall is in Latin. "His fame shall be more durable than rock. Nor shall future ages less than the present admire a soldier so pious and a minister so intrepid."

Nevertheless, Walker's other monument, a huge pillar erected on the Walls of Derry near St Augustine's church and overlooking the Bogside, was blown up in 1973.

STRABANE

Another man more associated with the city of Derry but also buried in County Tyrone was the so-called **Half Hanged MacNaghten** (1722–1761). John MacNaghten inherited his family estate at Benvarden in Derry when he was only eighteen years of age but squandered the lot on gambling. He then expediently married a young heiress, Sophie Daniel, but continued to amass huge gambling debts. When the sheriff burst into his house to take him into custody, his wife was killed in the commotion. To lose one wife in such circumstances would be bad enough but worse was to come . . . MacNaghten began to court Mary Anne Knox, the fifteen-year-old niece of Andrew Knox, MP for Donegal. He certainly knew that she would receive a marriage settlement of £6,000 – or perhaps he was genuinely in love with her. Despite Knox's opposition, MacNaghten and Mary Anne went through a secret marriage service. The Knox family went to court to have the marriage declared invalid. Despite losing the case, MacNaghten was determined to reclaim his bride. In November 1761, he and an accomplice ambushed the coach in which Mary Anne, her uncle and other family and servants were travelling to Dublin. Once again, in the fracas and commotion, MacNaghten's second wife was killed. After a period on the run with a price of 100 guineas on his head, he was captured hiding out in the hayloft of a local bleacher, charged with murder and sentenced to execution by hanging at Lifford.

MacNaghten had by then acquired popular and romantic status and no local man was prepared to erect a gallows or act as executioner. A hangman from outside the area was duly brought in. MacNaghten mounted the gallows, still protesting his love for Mary Anne and his innocence of her murder, put the rope around his own neck and jumped. The rope broke. MacNaghten could easily have escaped. Instead, he re-mounted the gallows, declaring that he did not wish to spend the rest of his life known as "Half-hanged MacNaghten", waited for another rope to be procured and was hanged at the second attempt. He was buried in St Patrick St Church in Strabane where an upright stone pillar marks his grave. Since then of course he has never been known as anything other than "Half-hanged MacNaghten."

Drumragh

Drumragh Church, a few miles outside Omagh, is the burial-place of the poet and republican, **Alice Milligan** (1866–1953). Milligan belonged to a wealthy Protestant family, the daughter of the antiquarian Seaton Milligan with whom she wrote a tourist guide, *Glimpses of Erin*, (1888). She went to Dublin to study Irish, attended meetings to hear Parnell speak and got to know Michael Davitt, William Butler Yeats and other members of the Gaelic League, for which she became a leading organiser. From 1896–1899 she edited the magazine *Shan Van Vocht* which enjoyed a wide circulation and published articles by James Connolly and Douglas Hyde. In 1898 she was secretary of the centenary celebrations for the 1798 United Irishmen Rebellion. She played no part in the 1916 Rising but, as a friend of Roger Casement, corresponded with him during his imprisonment and court-martial and was present outside the jail when he was hanged. She outlived all her contemporaries, her role in the late nineteenth century forgotten. She died alone in poverty. Her grave is at the rear left hand corner in a railed family plot. The headstone declares in Irish and English that she loved no other place but Ireland, and unfortunately, for no other reason, has been vandalised.

Barker, Juliet: *The Brontes* (Weidenfield & Nicolson 1994)

Barter, Richard: *The Rise and Progress of the Irish Graffenberg, Blarney. A lecture delivered at Bradford by Dr Barter on the improved Turkish Bath (1858)* (Routledge n.d.)

Bax, Arnold: *Farewell, my youth.* (Longmans 1943)

Beckett, JC: *The Making of Modern Ireland 1603–1923* (Faber and Faber London 1966)

Belfast Newsletter

Bowen, Desmond: *Souperism: Myth or Reality* (Cork Mercier Press 1970)

Bowen, Elizabeth: *Bowen's Court* (Longmans, Green & Co. 1942)

Boylan, Henry (ed): *A Dictionary of Irish Biography* (Gill & Macmillan Dublin 1978)

Bulfin, William: *Rambles in Eirinn* (Dublin Gill 1907)

Cantwell, Brian: *Memorials of the Dead* (Greystones 1990)

Chambers, Anne: *Granuaile, the life and times of Grace O'Malley* (Wolfhound 1979)

Collis, Maurice: *Somerville & Ross A Biography* (London Faber & Faber 1968)

Conlon, L: *The Heritage of Collon 1764-1984* [n.pub] 1984

Cork Examiner

Corkery, Daniel: *The Hidden Ireland* (Dublin Gill 1925)

Currie, JRL: *The Runaway Train* (David & Charles 1971)

Darinah, Boyle: *Half-Hanged MacNaghten* (Guildhall Press Derry 1993)

Dickson, Charles: *The Life of Michael Dwyer* (Richmond Press Dublin 1944)

Dictionary of National Biography: Edited Leslie Stephen and Sidney Lee (66 vols. London 1885–1901)

Dictionary of Ulster Biography: Edited Kate Newmann (Institute of Irish Studies Queen's University Belfast 1993)

Dinan, Brian: *Clare and its People, a concise history* (Mercier 1987)

Directory of Graveyards in the Dublin area (an index and guide to burial records) 2nd edition (Dublin Public Libraries 1990)

Donegal Democrat

Dublin University Magazine Vol. 18 (Dublin 1841)

Edgeworth, Maria: *Life and Letters of . . .* (Edward Arnold, London 1824)

Edgeworth, Richard Lovell: *Memoirs of . . . (Begun by himself and concluded by his daughter Maria Edgeworth)* (2 vols. London 1821)

Egan & Flatman: *Memorials of the Dead: Dublin City & County* (IGRS Dublin 1990)

Fairley, J: *Irish Whales & Whaling* (Belfast Blackstaff 1981)

Feehan, John: *The Landscape of Slieve Bloom* (Dublin Blackwater 1979)

Fermanagh Times

Fitzgerald, Richard: *Eileen Hanly: The true history of the Colleen Bawn* (Tralee, Anvil 1963)

Fitz-Simon, Christopher: *The Boys: A Biography of Micheál MacLíammóir and Hilton Edwards* (Nick Hern Books London 1994)

Freeman's Journal

Furlong, Nicholas Fr: *John Murphy of Boolavogue* (Geography Publications Dublin 1991)

Gallagher, Frank: *The History of Landlordism in Donegal* (Ballyshannon, Donegal Democrat 1975)

Gallagher, Patrick: *My Story* (Templecrone Cooperative Society 1939)

Gibbings, Robert: *Lovely is the Lee* (Dent 1945)

Graves, AP: *To return to all that: an autobiography* (Jonathan Cape London 1930)

Gravestone Inscription Series (Belfast Ulster Historical Foundation 1968–)

Gravestone Inscriptions County Down: General Editor RSJ Clarke (Ulster Historical Foundation Publications)

Hall, Mr and Mrs SC: *Ireland: Its scenery, Character etc.* (3 vols. London 1842)

Harbison, Peter: *Guide to the National Monuments in the Republic of Ireland* (Gill & Macmillan Dublin 1970)

Hardwick, Joan: *The Yeats Sisters, a biography of Susan and Elizabeth* (HarperCollins 1996)

Historic Monuments of Northern Ireland (HMSO Belfast 1983)

History Ireland

Holt, Joseph: *Memoirs of Joseph Holt General of the Irish Rebels in 1798* Ed. T Crofton-Croker (London 1838)

Hyman, Louis: *The Jews in Ireland from earliest times to the year 1910* (Irish University Press 1972)

Ireland Eyewitness Travel Guides (Dorling Kindersley London 1995)

Irish Press

Irish Sword Vol VI no. 23 Dublin 1963

Irish Times

Journal of the Association for the Preservation of the Memorials of the Dead in Ireland 1909

Journal of the Cork Historical and Archaeological Society

Journal of the County Donegal Historical Society

Journal of the Kerry Archaeological and Historical Society

Journal of the Kildare Archaeological Society

Journal of the Louth Archaeological Society 1934 and 1938

Journal of the Royal Society of Antiquaries of Ireland (Rev. SJD Seymour: The Cock and the Pot) Vol 51 1921

Joyce, John: *Graiguenamanagh a town and its people* (Graignamanagh 1993)

Leadbetter, Mary: *The Annals of Ballitore* (Bell & Daldy London 1862)

Leitrim Journal 1868

Loudan, Jack: *O Rare Amanda! The life of Amanda McKittrick Ros* 2nd edition (1969)

Lyons, JB: *Brief Lives of Irish Doctors* (Dublin 1978)

Lyons, JB: *What did I die of? The Deaths of Parnell, Wilde, Synge and Other Literary Pathologies* (Lilliput Press 1991)

MacDonagh, Oliver: *O'Connell The life of Daniel O'Connell* (Weidenfeld & Nicolson 1991)

Macrory, Patrick: *The Siege of Derry* (Oxford University Press 1980)

Madden, RR: *The United Irishmen – their lives and times* (7 vols. London 1843–1846)

Matthews, James: *Voices: A Life of Frank O'Connor* (McClelland & Stewart Ltd. Canada 1983)

McCoy, Jack: *Ulster's Joan of Arc: an examination of the Betsy Gray story* (Belfast 1987)

McDonald, Theresa: *Achill: 5000 BC to 1900 AD* (IAS Publications 1992)

McBride, Jack: *A Traveller in the Glens* (Appletree Press 1979)

McLaughlin, Enda: *Memoir for the Wasp* (Glendale Press 1989)

Memorial Inscriptions of Deansgrange Cemetery (4 vols Dun Laoghaire Genealogical Society 1994)

Mitchel, John: *Jail Journal (1848–1853) with an introduction on Mitchel's life and literary work by Rev. T Corcoran* (Dublin Browne & Nolan n.d.)

Modern Irish Lives: Dictionary of 20th century biography: General ed. Louis McRedmond (Gill & Macmillan 1966)

Montague, H Patrick: *The Saints and Martyrs of Ireland* (Smythe 1981)

Reade, George: *Brief Chronicles of the Bible in England and Ireland* (Dublin, George Herbert 1866)

Rourke, John: *The Great Irish Famine 1874* (reprinted Dublin 1989)

Seoighe, Mainchín: *Portrait of Limerick* (London Robert Hale 1982)

Skinner, Knute: *A Close Sky Over Killaspuglonane* (Dolmen Press 1968)

Somerville-Large, Peter: *Irish Eccentrics* (Hamish Hamilton London 1975)

Spelissy, Sean and O'Brien, John: *Limerick: the rich land* (O'Brien Press 1989)

Stagles, Ray: *The Great Blasket Island Guide* (O'Brien Press 1989)

The Bell

The Course of Irish History: ed. TW Moody and FX Martin (Mercier Press Cork 1967)

The Donegal Annual

The Field Day Anthology of Irish Writing ed. Seamus Deane 3 vols. Date of pub?

The Irish Digest

The Leitrim Guardian

The Old Limerick Journal

The Oxford Illustrated History of Ireland ed. RF Foster (Oxford 1989)

The Oxford Literary Guide to the British Isles ed. Dorothy Eagle & Hilary Carnell (Clarendon Press Oxford 1977)

Tierney, Mark: *Croke of Cashel* (Dublin, Gill & Macmillan 1976)

Tipperary Star

Ulster Journal of Archaeology

Waterford History and Society ed. William Nolan & Thomas P Power (Dublin Geography Publications 1992)

Webb, Alfred: *A compendium of Irish Biography* (London 1878)

Weekly Irish Times

Wilson, Gordon: *Marie: a story from Enniskillen* (London Collins 1990)

Woodham-Smith, Cecil: *The Great Hunger Ireland 1845–1849* (Penguin edition 1991)

INDEX